# Offline On Purpose

# Offline On Purpose

## Simple Habits to Break Screen Addiction and Take Back Your Time

Elias Ward

Mindful Pages

Published in 2025

ISBN: 9789371771641 (PB)
ISBN: 9789371777261 (eBook)

*Published by*

**Mindful Pages**
*Imprint of Alpha Editions LLC*
312 W. 2nd St #1834
Casper, WY 82601, USA


This book was developed using advanced writing tools to support the drafting and ideation process. All content has been thoughtfully curated, refined, and reviewed to ensure quality and relevance.

# Content

# Introduction
# The Hidden Cost of Convenience

We did not volunteer for this. The gradual colonisation of our attention was not orchestrated, but drifted into being—an unconscious slide into lives increasingly mediated by screens, alerts, and algorithms. Few of us deliberately chose to spend mornings scrolling, meetings multitasking, or evenings numbed by endless feeds. And yet, here we are: wired in, always on, rarely present. Our devices hum with promise, yet somehow siphon away peace, clarity, and time.

Convenience, that modern talisman, has long been equated with progress. A smoother, faster, more efficient world—tap, swipe, order, respond. Each incremental gain seemed to buy a fragment of time, only for it to vanish again into a thousand digital interruptions. Somewhere along the line, we stopped asking: convenient for what?

This book is not a call to abandon technology. It is no ode to nostalgia, nor a demand for digital purity. Rather, it is an invitation: to think, to choose, to reclaim. To inhabit life offline intentionally—not out of rejection, but from awareness. Regaining control of attention does not require retreat; it requires learning to inhabit the present more consciously.

The issue is not screen time itself. It is the quiet shaping of our inner lives by tools designed to bypass awareness. Every ping promises novelty; every scroll delivers stimulation. Resistance is no longer a matter of character but of design. The architecture of our digital lives is not neutral. It nudges, captures, converts attention into profit. And while this critique touches on the tech industry, it is first a reckoning with ourselves—with the unconscious choices we make, with hours surrendered unknowingly.

Modern life is engineered for engagement and against reflection. The result is a paradox: perpetually connected, yet profoundly distracted. Days fill with content but empty of presence. We know more, yet reflect less. We communicate constantly, yet often fail to feel seen. In this cognitive haze, we lose something vital—not only time, but agency: the ability to choose how we live, what we notice, and who we become.

*Offline On Purpose* does not aim to scare or shame. It is not a self-help diatribe of productivity hacks or morning routines. Instead, it offers a grounded framework for reshaping our relationship with technology: through design, intention, and awareness. We will not start by telling you to put your phone down—we begin by helping you see why you reach for it.

The book unfolds in layers, each chapter deepening understanding of how habits form—and how they can be reformed. First, we examine the invisible mechanisms governing compulsive use: persuasive design, attention hijacking, and the psychological loops keeping us scrolling. We trace technology's evolution from a tool to a total environment, blurring boundaries between work and rest, attention and distraction, connection and surveillance.

But critique alone is insufficient. From there, the focus turns to transformation. You will learn to discern necessary use from addictive behaviour, to design digital spaces that promote intention over impulse, and to build boundaries that feel liberating rather than restrictive. You will discover why multitasking is a myth, why boredom is a hidden strength, and how default settings may shape the defaults of your mind.

The aim is not to strip life of technology. It is to restore authority over it. To become the person who uses tech without being used. To protect attention not because it is fragile, but because it is foundational. Attention is not simply given away; it is the medium through which life is experienced. What you attend to shapes what you value; what you value shapes who you become.

The urgency is cultural as well as personal. Screen addiction is not merely a private inconvenience—it is a societal condition, influencing how we parent, partner, learn, lead, and relate. In a world equating busyness with worth and stimulation with meaning, reclaiming focus becomes resistance: quiet, sustained, deliberate—not dramatic, not heroic.

Behaviour change is difficult, particularly when pitted against systems optimised to override instincts. But change is possible—not through sheer will, but through redesigning the environments in which habits take root. Understanding frictionless design allows the introduction of purposeful friction. Recognising dopamine loops allows the creation of rituals that anchor us in deeper values. Seeing ourselves as out-designed, rather than weak, opens a new path: clarity, awareness, agency.

Each chapter moves from awareness to action, weaving stories, research, psychological models, and practical strategies. More importantly, you encounter yourself—habits, defaults, and hidden negotiations with attention. There is no single prescription, no linear route. What is universal is this: attention is finite. Time is non-renewable. The life you desire depends on how you steward both.

You will not be asked to renounce technology. You will be asked to rethink it. To disentangle convenience from compulsion. To move from autopilot to intention. Presence is not a relic of the pre-digital era—it is a skill, a discipline, a gift still cultivable today.

No need to abandon phones, delete accounts, or retreat to the wilderness. Begin by paying attention—on purpose, with purpose. Begin by living a little more awake.

The hidden cost of convenience is not mere distraction; it is the slow erosion of self. But that cost is not immutable. It can be reclaimed, starting with one deliberate, subversive, and powerful act: to go offline—on purpose.

# Chapter 1
# The Trap We Didn't See

Some traps do not snap shut suddenly. They creep in, imperceptible, until the moment arrives when choice feels suspended, replaced by reaction. What once seemed a helpful tool gradually asserts itself as a governor of daily life. This is the essence of the attention trap. It rarely announces itself with drama; it settles quietly, reshaping thought, behaviour, and social interaction. The truly disquieting aspect is that most of us scarcely notice it happening.

In the early days of digital innovation, technology appeared as a liberating force. A search bar that could answer any question. An email client supplanting cumbersome post. A device that combined calculator, map, music player, camera, bank, diary. Elegant. Efficient. Useful. Few paused to ask the deeper question: what is the long-term cost of making everything instantly accessible? Convenience was embraced with scarcely a thought of consequence. The architecture of our digital lives was not crafted with our wellbeing in mind, but for scale, speed, and shareholder returns.

To perceive the trap fully, we must acknowledge a profound shift: we are no longer mere users of technology—we are products within a market we rarely see. This is the attention economy. It is not simply that attention is valuable; it is that attention is being traded. Platforms profit not from your satisfaction, but from your engagement. The longer you linger, the more ads appear, the more data is collected, the more predictable and monetisable your behaviour becomes. The goal is not to improve life, but to capture your gaze and hold it.

Once this is understood, the moral calculus changes. Losing hours to screens is not weakness or laziness. We are contending with design systems engineered to exploit cognitive vulnerabilities. Persuasive technology, grounded in behavioural psychology, uses triggers, feedback loops, and variable rewards to shape behaviour. Consider the "pull to refresh" on social media—it mirrors a slot machine. The uncertainty, the intermittent reward, is addictive. Our brains are wired to repeat behaviours that occasionally gratify. This dopamine loop is foundational to habit formation.

Yet habit is not born merely of chemical stimulus—it is situational. Picking up a phone at a red light, checking emails at the first twinge of boredom: these are responses to environmental cues, not conscious deliberation. Most of our actions are governed less by willpower than by context. Willpower, despite its mythic status in self-help, is fragile. Environment, by contrast, is enduring. Change the environment, and behaviour often follows; leave it intact, and even strong resolve falters.

The tech industry knows this instinctively. Platforms are designed for ubiquity and frictionlessness. The fewer steps between thought and action, the greater the engagement. Notifications intrude into previously idle moments—lift rides, queues, waiting rooms. And these are no ordinary alerts—they are carefully crafted to provoke urgency or anticipation. The red dot on an app icon is calculated to demand action. Auto-play is not mere convenience; it is inertia engineered into the interface.

Over time, technology has shifted from tool to environment. Tools are optional, task-specific. Environments are omnipresent, ambient. We no longer "go online"—we are always online. Devices rarely leave our reach, and their influence permeates relationships, work, and even sleep. Boundaries between work and rest, public and private, solitude and connection, have eroded. Emails arrive at 10 p.m. expecting immediate acknowledgment. Screens are woven into daily life so thoroughly that absence feels deprivation. This is no longer dependence—it is entanglement.

Not all screen time is equal. Equating all usage with addiction is misleading. There is a distinction between instrumental and compulsive use. Checking a calendar, researching, video-calling a friend: purposeful. Unconscious feed-refreshing, habitual phone unlocking, anxiety when separated from a device: signs of behavioural drift. The question is not how long you spend on screens, but why, and how you feel when you stop.

Compulsive use often masquerades as productivity, as staying informed, as keeping up. Addiction does not always look dysfunctional. When technology ceases to serve priorities and begins to dictate them, that is the line to recognise.

Why is resisting so difficult? Because friction has been removed. In the analogue world, natural pauses existed—turning a page, waiting for a programme, walking to the store. Those moments allowed awareness to catch up with action. Digital life erases these seams. Everything is now, and everything is next. Mental punctuation—those pauses where choice emerges—is lost.

Paradoxically, seamless design makes self-control harder. Reflection is squeezed out between cue and response. Behaviour change relying solely on grit is doomed unless the environment prompting the behaviour is addressed.

This chapter will explore the architecture of digital compulsion. We will examine persuasive technologies, from variable rewards to dopamine-driven feedback loops, and the neuroscience underpinning them. We will trace the shift from tool to environment, and how this subtly remaps attention and time. The myth of willpower will be confronted, replaced with a more nuanced understanding of how behaviour is shaped—and can be reshaped—by design.

The objective is not guilt or shame, but comprehension. To reclaim attention, one must first understand how it was captured. The trap, once invisible, is now in plain view. The next step: stepping out—not by rejecting the digital world, but by redesigning one's relationship with it from the ground up.

Ultimately, the goal is simple, yet profound: to become not a passive participant, but the architect of your digital life. To see the systems, so you might shape them. Not for nostalgia, not for imagined purity, but because attention, once lost, cannot be reclaimed by accident. It must be reclaimed—on purpose.

## The Attention Economy and How It Hijacked You

The most valuable resource in the 21st century is not oil, data, or time—it is human attention. Not in the abstract, but in the most intimate sense: your capacity to focus, to direct thought, to make choices undistracted by noise. This is what the modern digital economy trades in. Not just what you click, but the mere fact that you are looking. In this ecosystem, attention is extracted, not offered. It is cultivated by design and harvested by architecture. And the troubling part is this: it is done with remarkable success, often without your awareness, and with very little resistance.

At the heart of this transformation is a convergence of behavioural psychology, interface design, and commercial incentive. Technology platforms have evolved from offering useful tools into creating immersive environments—closed loops that absorb attention, reward impulsivity, and normalise compulsion. What was once a web of information is now a net for your mind. And understanding how this system operates is the first act of reclaiming agency within it.

The design of modern platforms is not haphazard. It is the product of intensive research, iteration, and intentional manipulation of behavioural principles—much of it drawn from persuasive technology, a discipline born at Stanford's Behaviour Design Lab and now deeply embedded in Silicon Valley's DNA. Every interface you interact with—be it social media, streaming services, shopping platforms, or news aggregators—relies on a similar cognitive grammar. These interfaces are not neutral. They are loaded with triggers, feedback loops, and reward structures meticulously designed to prolong engagement.

Consider the concept of *variable rewards*, perhaps the most potent lever in the attention engineer's toolkit. Unlike predictable feedback, which soon loses its impact, variable rewards create a loop of anticipation and surprise. Scroll through a feed, and you might see something interesting—or you might not. That uncertainty is addictive. It mirrors the mechanics of gambling: a small input (a swipe, a click) with the potential for a psychological payout. The content doesn't have to be exceptional—it only has to be unpredictable. This intermittent reinforcement is powerful enough to override satiety, fatigue, even logic. Your brain learns to keep checking, not because the last hit was rewarding, but because the next one *might* be.

This is not simply about dopamine in the brain—though dopamine does play a central role. It's about the behavioural conditioning of attention. Platforms use small nudges to train users into habits that benefit the platform's engagement metrics. Notifications are not merely informative; they are stimuli designed to provoke action. The colour red for badges is not aesthetic; it is a psychological trigger optimised for urgency. Autoplay is not convenience; it is continuity designed to reduce decision points and prolong viewing. Every design choice has a purpose, and that purpose is rarely your wellbeing.

The brilliance—and danger—of this system is its subtlety. Rarely are we coerced. More often, we are nudged. And nudges, unlike commands, don't feel intrusive. They feel like features. Over time, you begin to expect them, then depend on them. You check your phone not because you consciously want to, but because it's become a reflexive response to boredom, uncertainty, or even just a momentary pause in conversation. This is behavioural capture, not by brute force, but by frictionless design.

What makes this environment so effective at hijacking attention is that it aligns the commercial interests of platforms with the unconscious patterns of human psychology. Unlike tools of the past—wrenches, typewriters, calculators—modern platforms evolve based on how you behave. Machine learning algorithms optimise your feed based on your previous clicks, scroll speed, watch time, and hesitation. In effect, you are training the system while the system is training you. This dynamic produces an *adaptive loop*, where the product becomes better at extracting your attention the more you use it.

And this extraction is no small matter. The average adult now checks their phone over 80 times per day. That is not idle curiosity—it is design manifesting as behaviour. Each glance may feel insignificant, but attention, like water, erodes with every trickle. Fragmentation becomes the new norm. Depth gives way to reaction. Focus is replaced by perpetual scanning. You are not simply using the technology—you are being shaped by it.

To understand the scale of this transformation, it's helpful to reflect on what has changed in the nature of attention itself. Historically, attention was a byproduct of interest and intention. You looked where you chose to look. You read what you wanted to understand. Now, attention is increasingly pulled rather than placed. It is allocated by algorithms and diverted by design. The locus of control has shifted—from the user to the system, from the individual to the interface.

This shift is not benign. It alters the very conditions under which thought, memory, and emotion occur. A constant influx of stimuli undermines not just focus, but *meta-cognition*—your ability to think about your thinking. When your attention is repeatedly fragmented, your awareness narrows. You become reactive, impulsive, easy to steer. In a sense, you lose the quiet space in which autonomy resides.

Yet for all its sophistication, the attention economy is not infallible. Its power depends on your participation. And that participation often rests on a misunderstanding—that the platforms you use are simply neutral spaces in which you browse, connect, or consume. In reality, they are immersive environments optimised to extract maximum dwell time. They do not wait passively for your engagement; they cultivate it. They do not merely respond to your interests; they *shape* them.

One of the most dangerous misconceptions is that spending time on screens is simply a matter of choice—that if you're distracted, it's because you lack discipline. But this places responsibility solely on the individual while ignoring the asymmetry of the system. You are not contending with a static object. You are contending with a dynamic, adaptive system that is designed to know more about your behaviour than you do. Willpower, in such a context, is not just insufficient—it is the wrong framework entirely.

The more constructive model is environmental. Instead of asking *why don't I have more discipline?*, the better question is *how is this environment shaping my behaviour without my consent?* This reframing opens the door to practical interventions. By understanding the architecture of persuasive technology, you can begin to reintroduce friction where platforms have removed it. You can create pauses, insert constraints, and reduce triggers—not to abstain from technology, but to restore intention within it.

The goal is not digital abstinence. That would be both unrealistic and unnecessary. The goal is sovereignty—the ability to use technology without being used by it. This requires recognising that your attention is not just something you give—it is something that can be taken. And once you see how it is taken, you can begin to protect it.

Consider the implications beyond individual usage. The collective impact of an attention-extractive economy is profound. When millions of people are nudged toward immediacy over reflection, novelty over understanding, stimulation over connection, the cultural cost is high. We lose depth in public discourse, patience in relationships, and presence in the moments that matter. The most precious things in life—clarity, intimacy, creativity—require uninterrupted time and undivided focus. When attention is splintered, these become harder to attain, not just individually, but socially.

Resisting the attention economy, then, is not simply a matter of personal wellbeing. It is a cultural necessity. But resistance does not begin with rage or retreat. It begins with comprehension. When you understand how persuasive design exploits your cognitive patterns, when you see how variable rewards keep you in the loop, when you recognise how your behaviours are being subtly shaped by systems optimised for engagement—you begin to regain your footing.

From that position, you can start to build alternatives. You can choose tools that serve your intentions rather than hijack them. You can adjust your environment to make mindful use easier and mindless scrolling harder. You can set boundaries—not as walls, but as guardrails that protect your most valuable asset: the capacity to direct your life with clarity and intention.

There is no final liberation from technology, nor should there be. But there is a path to using it with discernment. That path begins by seeing the attention economy not as an abstract force, but as a tangible architecture—one that you can learn to navigate, interrupt, and redesign. The cost of not doing so is high—not because technology is evil, but because it is powerful. And power, when left unexamined, always finds a way to shape us. Whether we notice or not.

## From Tools to Tyrants

The defining shift of the digital age is not that we use more technology, but that we live *inside* it. What began as a suite of external tools—discrete, purpose-built instruments we operated—has evolved into a full-spectrum environment. It surrounds us, shapes our routines, dictates our rhythms. The transformation from tool to environment was not heralded by a single event or product, but by a gradual encroachment of design into the margins of life—until the margins disappeared. We no longer log on; we *exist online.* The distinction between user and medium has blurred. And in that blurring, something vital has been lost: the boundary between intention and inertia.

Historically, tools served our ends. A hammer, a typewriter, a rotary phone—each had a defined function, a clear on-and-off state, and no motive of its own. They required our input, waited for our attention, respected our time. Early digital technologies, too, retained this posture. A word processor mirrored the typewriter. Email replaced letters and fax. The browser opened a window to information, but did not flood your workspace uninvited. Each tool had its role; none assumed total presence. The user was in control. But this structure began to break the moment technologies started integrating, learning, and responding—not to our declared goals, but to our observed behaviours.

The smartphone marked the turning point. Not because it introduced something fundamentally new, but because it combined everything old into a single, always-available gateway. The device itself is not the tyrant—it is the platform for an environment that never sleeps. It doesn't just hold your calendar and contacts; it holds your conversations, your media, your shopping, your banking, your news, your memories. It is the control centre for your social life and your professional identity. And crucially, it does not wait for you to summon it. It buzzes, flashes, nudges. It insinuates itself into meals, meetings, moments of silence. The tool has gained initiative.

This initiative is not random—it is systemic. Tech platforms have redefined themselves from service providers to ecosystems. A single company may own your messaging app, your social network, your file storage, and your digital wallet. These services are not merely connected; they are *interwoven.* Each interaction generates data that feeds back into the system, refining how it responds to you, predicts you, engages you. You no longer visit websites to complete tasks; you inhabit an environment designed to elicit perpetual interaction. The platform doesn't want you to leave—it wants you to *stay*, even when you've forgotten why you came.

This shift is subtle in form but sweeping in consequence. It has collapsed the natural boundaries that once structured human experience. Time that was once partitioned—work time, rest time, social time—now blurs into an undifferentiated stream of availability. Emails arrive in bed. Slack messages ping during dinner. Work documents are reviewed on holiday. The architecture of digital environments promotes continuity over closure. There is always another comment, another headline, another notification. The day has no edges.

These collapsed boundaries affect more than scheduling—they erode the psychological distinctions between roles. You are a professional, a parent, a friend, a citizen—but when these roles converge on the same screen, they begin to bleed into each other. The self is fragmented across tabs and apps, each demanding a different tone, a different persona, a different level of vigilance. This fragmentation is not always conscious, but it is cumulative. You find yourself mentally shifting gears dozens of times an hour, responding not to inner priority but to outer stimulus. The platform dictates the flow.

And with this erosion comes fatigue—not simply the exhaustion of doing too much, but the deeper fatigue of being unable to locate yourself in your own life. Rest loses definition when your leisure is indistinguishable from your feed. Focus becomes fragile when your attention is held hostage by devices that do not recognise boundaries. Even solitude becomes performative when your private moments are constantly interrupted by the potential for visibility. The environment does not turn off. And neither, increasingly, do we.

This is not a call for moral panic, nor is it a romanticisation of the analogue past. The technological environment we inhabit has brought extraordinary benefits—connectivity, access, opportunity. But acknowledging these gains should not blind us to the cost of their context. When the environment becomes total, so too does its influence. The concern is not the presence of technology, but the absence of choice in how it shapes our daily experience. Tools you control can be empowering. Environments you cannot exit become defining.

One of the most deceptive aspects of this shift is that it masquerades as convenience. The platforms integrate. The systems sync. Your documents are always accessible. Your friends are always reachable. But convenience, once rare and valuable, has become ambient and expected. And in its ubiquity, it exerts a quiet pressure. The email answered at 10 p.m. sets the precedent. The message seen and not replied to becomes a breach of etiquette. The "last seen" timestamp creates a metric of availability. The environment teaches not only what is possible, but what is *normal.* And over time, normal becomes mandatory.

This is the tyranny—not of oppression, but of expectation. The expectation that you will be reachable. That you will respond. That you will consume, post, react, engage. The platform does not force this behaviour; it fosters it, until it becomes second nature. You no longer ask whether to engage—you simply do. The medium becomes the atmosphere. The interaction becomes the habit. The tool becomes the way of life.

Escaping this dynamic is not a matter of deletion or disconnection. It is a matter of *discernment.* To use technology without being consumed by its environment requires deliberate architecture of your own. It means reintroducing structure where the platform erodes it. It means separating roles, defining limits, creating rituals that reassert your agency. It means recognising when a tool has ceased to serve your purposes and begun to dictate them. And it means cultivating awareness—not just of your usage, but of the *context* that shapes your usage.

That context is not neutral. It is shaped by commercial logic, by design psychology, by data incentive. The systems you inhabit are optimised not for your wellbeing, but for your engagement. This does not make them malicious—it makes them misaligned. And that misalignment must be recognised if it is to be corrected. Otherwise, the erosion continues—not because you made a wrong choice, but because you never saw the environment in which the choices were made.

To reclaim boundaries in a boundaryless environment is a profound act of self-authorship. It begins not with rejection, but with recognition. The recognition that what you assumed was a helpful tool may now be shaping your thoughts, your time, your sense of self. That the digital world is not something you occasionally access—it is something that constantly *frames* you. And that frame must be seen before it can be redrawn. The line between use and submission is thinner than it seems. Knowing where it lies is the first step in walking it with intention.

## Screen Time ≠ Tech Addiction

The phrase *screen time* has become a catch-all metric in discussions about digital wellbeing, often cited as a proxy for overuse, distraction, or dependency. It is quantified in hours, displayed on dashboards, used as the basis for shame-laden conversations and parental controls. But time alone tells us very little. A surgeon consulting radiographic imagery, a writer drafting a manuscript, and a teenager endlessly looping short-form videos may all rack up identical screen hours—but their experiences, intentions, and outcomes could not be more different. The deeper issue is not *how long* we spend in front of screens, but *why*, *how*, and *what happens to us* as a result.

To equate screen time with tech addiction is to misunderstand both. It suggests that any extended engagement with digital media is pathological, when in reality, addiction is not defined by duration, but by *compulsion*, *impairment*, and *loss of control*. Addiction is not merely heavy use—it is usage that persists despite negative consequences, interferes with basic functioning, and resists self-regulation. In this sense, someone who spends four hours a day reading academic papers on a tablet may be functioning healthily, while someone who compulsively checks their phone for social media validation every ten minutes, even during meals, work, or sleep, may be caught in a destructive loop—regardless of total time.

This distinction is not semantic; it is diagnostic. Lumping all screen use under the umbrella of "problematic" creates two distortions. First, it undermines legitimate, purposeful engagement with technology. Second, and more dangerously, it masks the true psychological patterns of compulsive use, allowing them to remain hidden under the normalised umbrella of everyday behaviour. Most people don't identify as addicted, even when their actions bear the marks of dependency—because the environment has shifted so gradually that what once would have seemed excessive now feels routine.

The modern digital landscape has made it harder than ever to draw clean lines between what is necessary and what is compulsive. Work emails are checked on the same device used for entertainment. News is consumed in the same format as personal updates. Professional tools and attention traps coexist on the same interface. The design of most apps, platforms, and devices actively encourages this convergence. What starts as a task often morphs into a trance. You pick up your phone to check the weather—and find yourself, fifteen minutes later, watching video clips that have nothing to do with your initial intention. This drift is not incidental; it is engineered.

To recognise compulsive use, we must look beyond screen time and examine behavioural patterns. Ask: *Do I reach for my device without conscious intent? Do I feel anxious or irritable when unable to check it? Do I struggle to stop even when I know I should? Do I experience a sense of relief or escape when using certain apps? Do I find it difficult to recall what I've actually done online during large swathes of time?* These are not questions about productivity; they are questions about autonomy.

Autonomy is the axis around which healthy use revolves. The difference between tool and tether is not how many minutes you spend, but how freely you can walk away. Necessary use is intentional, bounded, and value-aligned. It supports your goals, reflects your priorities, and leaves you feeling effective, connected, or informed. Compulsive use is reactive, unbounded, and dissociative. It is often misaligned with intention, leaves you fatigued or numbed, and is typically followed by a vague sense of regret.

One reason this distinction is hard to maintain is because compulsive behaviours are often socially sanctioned. Constant availability is conflated with professionalism. Immediate response times are seen as responsiveness rather than overextension. Sharing content is equated with participation. The line between cultural norm and individual impulse gets blurred. What would be flagged as problematic in other contexts—say, checking a slot machine every few minutes—passes without notice when it takes the form of screen-checking in a meeting, during a walk, or even in the toilet stall.

Moreover, many of the symptoms of compulsive tech use mimic behaviours we previously associated with diligence: checking in, staying informed, being responsive. This makes compulsive patterns harder to identify because they masquerade as virtues. But the distinction lies in the *relationship* to the behaviour, not the behaviour itself. A person who chooses to spend a long stretch online to complete meaningful work is not addicted. A person who reflexively taps and scrolls throughout the day, struggling to remember *why* they even began, may be.

The design of most platforms compounds this problem. Infinite scroll, autoplay, and algorithmic feeds all remove natural stopping points. Unlike reading a book or watching a film—activities with defined beginnings and endings—digital media offers no internal cues to pause. This continuity erodes self-regulation. In behavioural psychology, such design creates an *open loop*—a state in which actions are repeated because the system withholds clear cues for closure. In these conditions, users are not making free choices; they are reacting to cues embedded by design.

This context is essential in understanding why screen time is a blunt instrument for assessing digital health. It tells you nothing about *quality*, *context*, or *agency*. Two people may spend the same amount of time on a device and walk away with entirely different cognitive and emotional states. One may feel energised and connected; the other, drained and irritable. The crucial difference is not quantitative, but qualitative: was the use *deliberate*? Was it aligned with personal values? Was it mentally nourishing, neutral, or depleting?

Even the time of day plays a role. Research from cognitive neuroscience shows that screen exposure, particularly late at night, disrupts circadian rhythms and sleep architecture—especially when the use involves emotionally arousing content or blue light emission. Passive consumption before bed, often rationalised as unwinding, can have a paradoxical effect: heightening anxiety, delaying REM onset, and reducing sleep quality. This suggests that *when* and *how* screens are used matters as much as *how long*.

Age, context, and purpose also introduce critical distinctions. For example, a child spending two hours video-calling grandparents and another two hours gaming is engaging in profoundly different cognitive and emotional activities. The first strengthens relational bonds; the second may or may not offer psychological nourishment, depending on content, pacing, and personal temperament. Likewise, a remote worker attending virtual meetings should not be lumped into the same evaluative frame as someone binge-watching videos alone out of boredom or emotional avoidance.

Cultural assumptions further complicate the discussion. Western societies, particularly in professional and urban contexts, valorise digital fluency. Constant connectivity is seen not just as competence, but as an expression of ambition. This distorts our perception of tech use. Someone glued to their screen at a café may be seen as productive rather than compulsive. The underlying anxiety, avoidance, or habit loop remains invisible behind the veneer of activity. In this context, addiction hides in plain sight.

To navigate this complexity, what is needed is a new diagnostic lens—one that shifts the focus from *how much* to *how mindfully*. This lens does not demonise screen use, nor does it valorise abstinence. It invites honest reflection on the lived experience of digital engagement. What feelings precede your device use? What states follow? Are you escaping, connecting, creating, distracting? Do your habits reflect what you *value*, or what you have come to tolerate?

Ultimately, digital wellbeing cannot be measured in hours alone. It must be measured in *alignment*: the extent to which your tech use serves your chosen goals rather than subverting them. Compulsive use hijacks intention. It replaces self-directed action with reactive behaviour. It creates the illusion of choice while narrowing your cognitive and emotional range. This is why reclaiming digital agency requires more than screen limits—it requires pattern recognition, context design, and inner clarity.

The path forward is not technophobia, nor blind embrace. It is precision. Learn to distinguish the productive from the compulsive, the necessary from the automatic, the enriching from the numbing. Replace the question *How much screen time is too much?* with *Is my screen time chosen or conditioned?* This is the more difficult question—but also the more transformative. Because it shifts the focus from control to consciousness. And from that consciousness, new habits, new rhythms, and new relationships with technology can emerge. Not imposed. Not enforced. But chosen—with clarity, and on purpose.

## Why Willpower Fails

It is one of the most resilient myths of modern self-improvement: that if you truly cared enough, tried hard enough, or simply applied more willpower, you could control your tech habits. That if you just had better discipline, you'd stop checking your phone before bed, resist the urge to scroll during meetings, and avoid that afternoon rabbit hole of feeds and forums. This belief—that behaviour is primarily a function of personal resolve—has become so embedded in our cultural psyche that failing to "stay off the screen" feels like a personal weakness. But the science tells a different story, and it begins with this critical insight: *in an environment designed for frictionless engagement, willpower is a poor tool for resistance.*

The human capacity for self-control, while real, is limited. The brain's executive functions—particularly those involving impulse control, delayed gratification, and attention regulation—draw heavily on cognitive resources. These resources are finite. The more decisions you are forced to make, the more fatigued your system becomes, a phenomenon known in behavioural psychology as *decision fatigue*. In environments that present frequent, low-friction opportunities for distraction, these micro-decisions accumulate rapidly. Each ignored ping, each resisted urge to check a notification, each attempt to return to focus requires an act of will. Over time, the cognitive cost adds up, and resistance weakens—not because you are flawed, but because the architecture is rigged for depletion.

Unlike traditional temptations, which often reside in specific times or places—a cigarette, a drink, a dessert—the digital environment is omnipresent. The smartphone, for example, is not just a device; it is a portal to countless options: news, messages, games, content, shopping, validation. And each of these options is available instantly, seamlessly, and often for free. The very concept of *friction*—that natural pause or cost that might interrupt a compulsion—has been systematically designed out. You don't have to go somewhere to engage; you simply *tap*. And once inside, the system is designed to keep you there. Infinite scroll, autoplay, push alerts, and AI-curated feeds work not against your will, but around it.

This frictionless design exploits what behavioural economists call *present bias*—the tendency to prioritise immediate rewards over long-term outcomes. Every time you reach for your phone during a difficult task or uncomfortable emotion, you're rewarded with novelty, stimulation, or escape. The consequences—lost time, diminished focus, emotional residue—are delayed and abstract. In this equation, the moment always wins. And no amount of moralising about willpower will override a neurological system built to prioritise short-term pleasure when no structural barriers stand in the way.

Consider the analogy of a buffet. If you are surrounded by ultra-palatable, high-calorie food, presented in an appealing, always-available format, it is not your lack of discipline that drives you to overeat—it is the environment. Behavioural cues—smell, sight, availability—trigger consumption that is far harder to regulate than when those same foods are less visible or more difficult to access. In a similar way, digital environments have removed the "containers" that once protected our attention. We no longer wait for a programme to air or for a letter to arrive. Everything is immediate, embedded, and personalised. There is no stopping point unless you create one.

This is why interventions that rely solely on personal resolve tend to fail. Studies on behaviour change, from addiction recovery to dietary improvement, consistently show that *context beats character.* Environments that support desirable behaviour make change sustainable. Those that undermine it—even subtly—render change fragile. The classic study by Wendy Wood and David Neal at Duke University found that around 40 percent of daily actions are not decisions, but *habits*—automated behaviours triggered by context. If you sit on the same couch, at the same time of day, with the same device in hand, your brain does not pause to ask what the best use of your time is. It repeats the familiar loop. Willpower is bypassed entirely.

The fallacy of relying on willpower also ignores the strategic sophistication of the systems we are up against. These platforms employ teams of behavioural scientists, attention economists, and interface designers whose job is to make staying engaged feel effortless and exiting feel like effort. From haptic feedback to personalised algorithms, every element is optimised for *stickiness*. If resisting this pull feels like swimming against a current, that's because it is. And the current is not accidental—it is profit-driven.

This has ethical implications. When people are told to "just log off" or "try harder," the burden of responsibility shifts entirely to the individual. This framing absolves platforms from accountability and conceals the engineered nature of the compulsion. It is the digital equivalent of telling someone in a casino to just stop playing, while the lights, sounds, and free drinks continue unabated. True agency requires more than internal resolve; it requires an environment that does not actively erode resolve in the first place.

So what does a more realistic model of behaviour change look like in this context? First, it requires acknowledging that *design matters*. Interfaces that insert even small amounts of friction—such as grayscale mode, notification batching, or removal of autoplay—can dramatically reduce compulsive engagement. Not because they force restraint, but because they create a moment of awareness: a gap between urge and action where intention can surface. These are not hacks; they are architectural choices that shift the default.

Second, behaviour change becomes more sustainable when we *design for defaults*. The brain is biased toward the path of least resistance. If the most visible, accessible, and easy-to-engage option is also the most aligned with your values, behaviour improves without requiring constant self-monitoring. This is why phone layouts, app organisation, and environmental cues matter. A home screen that centres tools for creation rather than consumption does not eliminate temptation—it makes a better choice easier to reach.

Third, context must be treated not as a backdrop, but as an active participant in behaviour. This means aligning physical space with mental intention. Workspaces should be designed to promote focus. Bedrooms should signal rest, not stimulation. Even small rituals—placing devices in a drawer, wearing headphones to signal deep work, or scheduling tech-free windows—can recalibrate the relationship between place and purpose. These contextual cues help re-establish the kind of boundaries that frictionless design has eroded.

Fourth, and perhaps most importantly, this model recognises that *self-control is relational*. People who succeed in managing their tech use often do so not through heroic effort, but through external scaffolding: accountability, shared norms, social contracts. Families that co-create tech rules tend to enforce them more consistently. Work teams that protect focus time reduce internal pressure to be always-on. Culture matters—not as an abstract construct, but as a practical framework that shapes what behaviour is normal, acceptable, and expected.

The shift from willpower to environment is not about absolving personal responsibility. It is about *situating responsibility accurately*. Your habits are not solely a reflection of your character. They are the product of thousands of contextual nudges, many of which operate below the threshold of conscious awareness. Until we see the system for what it is—an attention economy optimised for exploitation—we will continue to ask the wrong questions, blame ourselves for predictable failures, and attempt solutions that do not match the complexity of the problem.

Reclaiming attention, then, is not about becoming stronger. It is about becoming *strategic*. It means seeing self-regulation not as an internal resource to be summoned endlessly, but as a function of external alignment. It means recognising that better choices emerge more often not from better people, but from better systems. And it means understanding that discipline, while admirable, is not scalable. Design is.

If willpower has failed you, it is not because you lack it. It is because it was never meant to carry this load. The solution is not to double down on grit, but to redesign the ground beneath your feet. Because the most powerful behaviour change does not feel like a daily struggle. It feels like clarity. Like ease. Like making the right thing the default. And then choosing it—not out of will, but out of habit.

# Chapter 2
# The Myth of Staying Connected

We are more connected than ever—more people, more channels, more constantly—but this connectivity conceals a paradox: the very abundance of contact fragments our attention, dilutes our relationships, and often leaves us feeling more isolated. Our devices hum with digital life—notifications ping, updates roll in, conversations traverse continents in real time—but the emotional richness promised by this perpetual connection rarely materialises. Instead, a distracted mode of living has become normalised, where presence is traded for availability and engagement is measured in fleeting pings rather than meaningful interaction.

To begin, it must be said plainly: being always-on is not the same as being fully present. The two often pull against each other. Presence demands attention, and attention is finite. Every ping that diverts the gaze from someone in front of you, every compulsive glance at a feed mid-conversation, every micro-interruption that splinters focus draws you away not only from tasks, but from the moments themselves. Moments, once fragmented, lose density and weight; they vanish into forgettable blur. It is not that people matter less—it is that our capacity to engage meaningfully with them is eroded by the relentless demands of digital immediacy.

The effects ripple inward as well. Minds trained to flit between tabs, threads, and notifications grow increasingly uncomfortable with sustained attention—whether for deep work, reflection, or creative thought. The brief rush of a received message or an acknowledged post acts as a substitute for deeper satisfaction, yet the more we chase this stimulation as a proxy for connection, the hungrier we become. Loneliness is not born of physical isolation alone, but of relational shallowness. You can be surrounded by a chorus of digital voices and still feel profoundly alone if none of those interactions touches your inner world.

This confusion between stimulation and connection defines the psychological landscape of our age. We scroll not simply because we are lonely, but because the scroll mimics social proximity. We post not out of vanity, but because platforms train us to equate performance with presence. Likes, shares, and comments provide instantaneous, measurable feedback—but they lack the richness, subtlety, and context of genuine human exchange. Gradually, our sense of worth becomes calibrated not through reflection or conversation, but through dashboards of digital affirmation.

A subtler danger is the internalisation of surveillance. Platforms designed for sharing have become arenas of performance. Private thoughts once recorded in diaries are now curated posts; phone calls are often replaced by comment threads. Visibility has become a proxy for validity. The pressure to appear engaged and maintain an online presence shapes not only what we do, but how we see ourselves. We edit behaviours for traction rather than truth. This is not connection—it is conditioning.

Ironically, these tools began under the banner of authenticity: "Share your life," they promised, "stay close to those who matter." Yet their evolution has outpaced these intentions. Algorithms reward engagement, not intimacy. They privilege content that sparks reaction over reflection, nudging us toward extremes. Outrage travels faster than nuance; novelty keeps us returning. The architecture of these platforms is not neutral—it is engineered to sustain motion, often steering us away from the very connections that satisfy.

Withdrawal is not the solution. Digital exile is neither realistic nor necessary. What is required is a redefinition of connection itself—decoupling it from metrics of visibility and anchoring it in attention, empathy, presence, and depth. This is not nostalgia for analogue life; it is a deliberate recalibration. It involves recognising the difference between fleeting stimulation and real conversation, prioritising fewer but richer relationships, and embracing boredom as a portal to thought, creativity, and self-awareness that constant connectivity keeps at bay.

True connection requires friction. It cannot be rushed, gamified, or quantified. It grows in pauses between messages, in the silences of mutual understanding, in the continuity of shared history. It is sustaining rather than flashy, and it is these sustaining bonds—

personal, professional, internal—that give life its meaning. Without them, busyness may replace significance, and activity may masquerade as engagement.

Throughout this chapter, we will explore how the seductive pull of connectivity contrasts with the deeper rewards of presence. We will examine how platforms, despite promising community, can produce distraction, fatigue, and performance pressure. Psychological mechanisms that make shallow engagement compelling will be unpacked, alongside practical, research-informed strategies for cultivating depth. This is not about reducing screen time per se; it is about restoring integrity to attention and authenticity to interactions.

Perfection is not the goal. Phones will still be used, messages still exchanged, online life still entered. But the hope is that engagement occurs with greater consciousness—clarity about what you seek and what you will protect. Real connection does not happen automatically. It must be cultivated, safeguarded, chosen. In a world demanding attention at every turn, choosing depth is not default—it is a deliberate act, renewed moment by moment, with purpose.

## Always-On, Rarely Present

There is a fundamental mismatch between the pace of digital communication and the requirements of human presence. The former thrives on speed, frequency, and availability; the latter demands slowness, depth, and attention. Yet in recent years, the two have become conflated. We are told that to be connected is to be engaged, that to be reachable is to be involved, that the more we respond, the more we belong. But the lived experience of this logic tells another story—one in which we are everywhere, yet seldom *with* anyone, including ourselves. Constant connectivity, far from enhancing human experience, has made our attention more fragmented, our relationships more superficial, and our engagement more brittle.

The defining feature of the digital environment is that it never turns off. Unlike physical spaces, which close for the night, or broadcast television, which once followed programming schedules, the internet operates in a state of perpetual availability. Emails arrive at midnight. Messages can be read and replied to while standing in queues, attending meetings, or sitting at dinner tables. Social platforms cycle endlessly, always updating, always refreshing, always suggesting. In this context, *rest* begins to look like *neglect*, *disconnection* like *absence*, and *slowness* like *incompetence*. The boundaries that once protected our mental space have dissolved.

The neurological implications are considerable. Human attention is not designed for perpetual vigilance. Cognitive science has long demonstrated that the brain operates best in cycles of focused effort and rest. The prefrontal cortex—the part responsible for planning, decision-making, and self-regulation—fatigues under continuous cognitive load. Interruptions, particularly those that carry emotional salience (a message from a colleague, a reaction to a post), create what researchers call *attention residue*—a lingering cognitive fragment that depletes bandwidth and delays the return to deep thought. The result is not just a momentary lapse in focus but a cumulative erosion of cognitive efficiency.

This erosion spills into our relationships. At the heart of meaningful connection is the ability to *attend to another person*, to listen fully, respond thoughtfully, and hold emotional space. These behaviours require undivided attention. But when devices are within reach—and especially when they are active—the attention we offer others becomes partial. Numerous studies in social psychology have shown that the mere *presence* of a smartphone on the table, even if untouched, reduces the perceived quality of conversation. It diminishes empathy, shortens responses, and signals divided priority. The person in front of you competes with the possibility of someone more interesting, urgent, or rewarding on the other side of the screen.

The cumulative impact of this divided presence is a thinning of relational quality. We check in more, but we understand less. We send more messages, but communicate less meaning. The frequency of contact masks a decline in emotional depth. People begin to feel vaguely unheard, subtly dismissed, or emotionally bypassed—not because the other person doesn't care, but because attention is repeatedly diverted elsewhere. Over time, these microfractures accumulate. Friendships feel performative. Romantic connection becomes strained. Parents become background noise in their own homes. And individuals start to internalise a belief that they are not compelling enough to hold someone's attention for long.

This phenomenon is compounded by workplace norms that valorise availability. The professional culture of many industries now operates under the unspoken assumption that responsiveness equals competence. Replying quickly, being always reachable, checking emails during non-working hours—these behaviours are increasingly rewarded, whether through praise or promotion. But the trade-off is steep. What looks like dedication often masks a lack of boundaries. Colleagues operate in a state of persistent partial focus, jumping between tasks, checking in during meetings, mentally toggling between the present conversation and the unread message in their inbox. This fragmentation not only undermines performance—it corrodes the experience of *being present at work*.

And then there is the personal cost: the toll of never fully unplugging. The inability to mentally disengage from messages, updates, or ongoing dialogues creates a condition psychologists refer to as *continuous partial attention*. Unlike multitasking, which juggles multiple tasks at once, continuous partial attention is a state of readiness to be interrupted. It is a hypervigilant posture of mind, where attention is not so much deployed as it is scattered—prepared to shift, but never fully settled. Over time, this state contributes to elevated stress, reduced creativity, and an impaired ability to enter flow states. In short, it leaves the mind always active but seldom satisfied.

The deeper issue is not merely behavioural, but existential. When attention is habitually fragmented, identity becomes unstable. One's inner life is no longer shaped through sustained reflection or uninterrupted experience but through a stream of reactions, alerts, and prompts. The self becomes reactive rather than reflective. Moments that once offered opportunities for integration—solitude, boredom, waiting—are now filled with content. But content is not contemplation. And in the absence of contemplation, the capacity to process, understand, and *be with* one's experience begins to atrophy.

This is where the promise of connectivity begins to collapse under its own weight. The tools that were meant to bring us closer—to loved ones, to information, to opportunity—are now the very mechanisms that displace us from ourselves and one another. The fantasy of being "always-on" has yielded a reality in which we are rarely *here*. The present moment, instead of being inhabited, is bypassed. We are elsewhere—in inboxes, in timelines, in peripheral alerts.

The solution lies not in rejecting connectivity outright, but in reframing it. Being available does not mean being present. The quality of our relationships—both with others and ourselves—is determined less by how often we check in and more by how fully we show up. Presence is not accidental. It is intentional. It requires the deliberate withdrawal from the constant buzz of elsewhere. It means choosing not to respond immediately, not to scroll reflexively, not to permit every ping to override the moment.

Creating the conditions for presence in a hyper-connected world requires more than discipline. It demands *design*. Devices must be configured to respect boundaries. Notifications must be curated, not tolerated. Digital spaces must be structured in ways that support focus, not fracture it. And above all, we must relearn the value of stillness—not as a luxury, but as a necessity. Because in stillness, we become available—not to the world, but to what is actually happening.

Always-on culture is not inevitable. It is constructed, encouraged, and reinforced by systems that benefit from our perpetual attention. But presence—true presence—is a choice. A deliberate, often inconvenient, and always meaningful choice. And it is only in presence that connection becomes real, attention becomes whole, and the self becomes coherent once again.

## Connection vs. Stimulation

The human need for connection is not a luxury or a personality trait—it is foundational. Across disciplines, from developmental psychology to neuroscience, the consensus is clear: to flourish, we must feel seen, heard, and meaningfully engaged with others. Yet in an age of constant digital stimulation, that need is often confused with something else entirely. A stream of pings, replies, likes, and reactions may *resemble* connection, but what they often deliver is a form of social stimulation—immediate, accessible, and largely superficial. This confusion is not harmless. It dilutes our understanding of what it means to belong, and worse, it leaves us lonelier than before, despite the illusion of togetherness.

The fundamental difference between connection and stimulation lies in depth and mutuality. *Connection* requires presence, vulnerability, and reciprocal engagement. It is slow, sometimes effortful, and inherently relational. *Stimulation*, on the other hand, is fast, transactional, and often one-directional. It gives the appearance of interaction while bypassing the emotional labour of real intimacy. A heart emoji, a double tap, a one-word reply—these gestures are not meaningless, but they are not substitutes for true attunement. They offer brief emotional spikes without the continuity that sustains closeness.

Digital platforms are not designed to foster connection in its deepest sense. They are designed to maximise engagement—measured not in quality, but in frequency. The more frequently users interact, the more time they spend on the platform; the more time they spend, the more valuable they become to advertisers. This creates a structural incentive to prioritise *low-friction, high-frequency exchanges* over meaningful conversation. As a result, we become habituated to shallow interaction. Checking our phones for updates becomes a reflex, not because the messages are meaningful, but because the act of checking delivers a hit of stimulation. Over time, the brain begins to mistake this stimulation for connection itself.

One of the most concerning aspects of this shift is its impact on emotional regulation. Human relationships are a primary mechanism through which we regulate affective states. We turn to others for comfort, affirmation, and perspective. But when stimulation replaces connection, the regulation becomes less interpersonal and more algorithmic. We scroll when anxious, refresh when bored, click when lonely—not to reach someone, but to distract ourselves from the discomfort of disconnection. And because these behaviours offer short-term relief, they become reinforcing. The more we rely on digital inputs to manage emotional states, the less tolerant we become of the ambiguity, slowness, or messiness that real connection entails.

This habituation also alters our expectations of others. When connection is filtered through platforms that reward immediacy and brevity, patience begins to feel like neglect. A delayed response is interpreted as disinterest. A nuanced conversation feels inefficient. The relational rhythm of digital life accelerates beyond what human cognition or emotion can sustainably match. And in this acceleration, we lose not only depth, but trust. The trust that others are with us, even when they are not signalling it constantly. The trust that presence need not be performative. The trust that quiet, sustained engagement counts—even when it isn't visible.

Confusing stimulation for connection also distorts our sense of relational fulfilment. It is entirely possible to be surrounded by digital interaction and feel profoundly alone. In fact, research increasingly shows a correlation between high social media use and increased feelings of loneliness—particularly when that use is passive or compulsive. The brain receives signals of social activity (faces, messages, likes), but without the embodied context, non-verbal cues, or shared experience that give those signals meaning. It is the social equivalent of eating ultra-processed food: calorie-dense but nutritionally empty. You are fed, but not nourished.

Real connection has a different texture. It emerges through presence, curiosity, and co-regulation. It involves risk—of misunderstanding, rejection, vulnerability. But it also builds resilience, empathy, and continuity. A shared silence with a friend, a difficult conversation with a partner, a moment of laughter that no one else witnessed—these are the fibres of connection. They are not designed. They are not optimised. They cannot be gamified. And that is precisely why they matter.

To recover connection in a world saturated with stimulation requires a deliberate shift in both mindset and practice. First, it demands that we re-evaluate the emotional signals we respond to. That momentary feeling of being noticed—the rush when someone likes your post or replies instantly—is not inherently bad. But if it becomes the primary mode of affirmation, it starts to eclipse deeper needs. Recognising the difference between being seen and being known is critical. The former is visible, frequent, and platform-driven. The latter is subtle, slow, and relationally anchored.

Second, we must create environments where connection can grow. This means protecting time and space from the constant intrusion of stimuli. It means choosing face-to-face over feed-to-feed where possible. It means embracing awkward pauses, messy conversations, and uncurated presence. Because these are the raw materials from which trust and intimacy are built. Digital convenience cannot replace the effort of showing up, emotionally and physically, for another person.

Third, we must retrain our attention. The attentional economy does not reward stillness or depth. It rewards reactivity. But connection does not unfold in reaction. It unfolds in sustained attention—attention that is not merely available, but invested. This may involve resisting the impulse to check a device during conversation, allowing for silence instead of filling space with content, or setting aside time for undistracted dialogue. These acts may seem minor, even quaint, but their cumulative effect is profound. They signal to others—and to ourselves—that presence matters more than novelty.

The final and perhaps most difficult shift is internal. It requires that we examine our own habits, not with guilt, but with curiosity. What needs are we trying to meet through stimulation? Is it loneliness, boredom, anxiety, validation? And might those needs be better met through slower, richer forms of engagement? The answers will vary. But the asking itself begins the process of realignment—from compulsive response to conscious choice.

Connection is not disappearing. It is being displaced. And that displacement is reversible, but only if we recognise the difference between what feeds our social reflexes and what nourishes our social selves. Confusing the two leaves us overstimulated and under-connected—busy but emotionally underfed, surrounded but unseen. To find our way back, we must be willing to choose less stimulation in exchange for more substance. Not always. Not perfectly. But consistently enough that connection can find its place again—not as a feature, but as a foundation.

## When Social Becomes Surveillance

Social media was not invented to make us feel watched. It arrived under the banner of openness and sharing—an invitation to connect, communicate, and express freely in digital space. But as platforms evolved, so too did their architecture, incentives, and psychological effects. What began as spontaneous self-expression has quietly morphed into something far more calculated: *performance under observation*. Over time, the design of these platforms has recast visibility as validation, metrics as meaning, and public exposure as the price of belonging. In this shift, something fundamental has changed: we are no longer just participating in social life online—we are performing it for an audience that is always there and never quite known.

To understand this transformation, it's necessary to examine how social platforms mediate identity. Social identity is, by nature, constructed and adaptive; we shift tone, language, and presentation depending on context. But in physical space, those contexts are bounded and mutually exclusive. You do not speak to your colleagues as you do your childhood friends or behave at a job interview as you would at home. Social media collapses these contexts into a single, undifferentiated stage. On this stage, we are aware—consciously or not—of being observed not just by friends, but by acquaintances, coworkers, employers, former classmates, and strangers. The result is a form of ambient surveillance, where the pressure to be perceived in a certain way subtly shapes what we share, how we behave, and even how we think about ourselves.

This ambient surveillance is not imposed by external monitoring in the traditional sense—it is internalised. Unlike CCTV or formal oversight, which involve clear observers and intentions, social media surveillance is psychological. The viewer is not a single entity but a shifting composite of imagined audiences: followers, lurkers, silent scrollers, people we haven't seen in years but who still watch our stories. We curate for them not because we are narcissistic, but because the platforms are built on visibility as currency. The incentive structures—likes, shares, comments, follower counts—encourage us to post what performs, not necessarily what's real.

The performance becomes most pronounced when content is explicitly personal. A vacation photo, a relationship milestone, a vulnerable reflection—these may feel authentic at the moment of posting, but their construction is rarely free from the influence of anticipated feedback. We consider what version of the story to tell, how it will be framed, whether it will resonate or fall flat. The desire to be seen is human, but on these platforms it becomes distorted by metrics. A moment shared with others quickly becomes a moment evaluated by others.

This evaluative loop has subtle but significant psychological effects. The self becomes increasingly tied to metrics that were never designed to reflect human complexity. A photo that receives more likes than usual doesn't merely signal popularity—it feeds into a feedback loop of self-assessment. You feel better, more validated, more visible. A post that goes unnoticed does the opposite—it induces doubt, insecurity, or the sense of being ignored. Over time, these feedback loops condition us to shape behaviour around visibility rather than authenticity. We begin to ask not *What matters to me?* but *What will get traction?*

This shift is not superficial. It has consequences for identity formation, especially among adolescents and young adults whose sense of self is still forming. Studies in developmental psychology have shown that identity consolidation depends heavily on exploration and feedback from trusted peers. But when that feedback is algorithmically distributed and publicly quantified, the process becomes skewed. Rather than being based on mutual engagement and trust, self-concept is increasingly influenced by platform dynamics: What gets likes? What content trends? What version of me is most legible to the algorithm?

Adults are not immune. The compulsion to present a coherent, polished version of one's life online extends into professional life, parenting, friendships, and even leisure. The boundary between the private and the performative dissolves. Experiences are filtered through the question of *shareability*. A sunset isn't simply admired; it is captured, edited, and captioned. A dinner with friends isn't just enjoyed; it is presented as proof of one's social vitality. These acts are not inherently disingenuous, but their accumulation creates a subtle detachment. Life becomes lived with an eye towards external perception.

The irony is that this hyper-visibility can coincide with a deepening sense of invisibility. When the dominant form of engagement is performance, the experience of being *known*—genuinely, intimately, without audience—becomes rare. Performative sharing invites reaction but often discourages reciprocal vulnerability. Comments and emojis replace conversations. The result is a paradoxical condition: publicly exposed, yet privately unseen. This can lead to a form of *social dysphoria*, where one feels out of sync with the persona being performed.

It is easy to misattribute these dynamics to individual choices. Why not just post less? Be more authentic? Ignore the metrics? But this overlooks the structural nature of the platforms themselves. They are not passive channels for communication; they are engineered systems that reward particular behaviours. The design nudges users toward engagement that is visible, measurable, and repeatable. Algorithms prioritise content that performs well according to specific parameters—engagement rates, view time, virality. Posts that provoke outrage or humour are promoted, while those that express ambiguity, complexity, or subtlety are often buried. Over time, users learn to shape their behaviour not by internal values but by external incentives.

This is where the concept of *platformed selfhood* becomes relevant. Sociologist Alice Marwick defines the platformed self as a mode of identity shaped by social media's affordances, algorithms, and audiences. It is a self that is always aware of being watched, always adjusting, always partially performed. Importantly, this self is not inauthentic—it is *adaptive*. But in adapting to a system that rewards surface and speed, depth and introspection are pushed aside.

The most troubling aspect of this adaptation is that it normalises surveillance as a mode of being. When we willingly submit to being constantly seen, and when our self-worth becomes tethered to the responses of others in public space, we participate in our own monitoring. The line between connection and compliance becomes blurred. We curate our lives not just to connect, but to conform—to aesthetic norms, ideological tribes, professional branding, lifestyle trends. The result is a narrowing of self-expression disguised as empowerment.

To reclaim authenticity in this context does not require withdrawing from social platforms entirely. Rather, it demands a more critical awareness of their structure and influence. It begins with recognising when performance has become default, when expression has been shaped more by anticipation than intention. It means asking: *Is this being shared to connect or to be seen? Does this post reflect me or perform me? Am I measuring my life by metrics that were never designed for meaning?*

Reconnection with authenticity also requires spaces where surveillance is suspended—where feedback is delayed, where sharing is optional, where presence matters more than performance. These might be private conversations, group chats, offline gatherings, or creative practices not designed for public consumption. They are rare, and they must be protected. Because in these spaces, identity is allowed to emerge unedited.

Social platforms have rewired the grammar of self-expression. They have made visibility a proxy for value and performance a stand-in for personhood. But the self cannot be sustained on metrics alone. It needs intimacy, complexity, and contradiction. And these things rarely perform well.

If we are to live well in digital environments, we must learn to distinguish between the kind of sociality that connects and the kind that performs. We must remember that not all exposure is expression, and not all visibility is validation. Surveillance begins when we stop asking who we are and start asking only how we appear. To resist this requires not withdrawal, but discernment—an insistence on bringing our whole selves into a system that prefers fragments. Not perfectly. But consciously. And often quietly.

## Choosing Depth in a Shallow World

The defining challenge of our time may not be technological overload, but depth deprivation. In a world designed for speed, brevity, and stimulation, the capacity to remain in one place—mentally, emotionally, or relationally—has become a rare and endangered skill. The structure of our digital environment rewards surface-level interaction: skimmed headlines, one-tap responses, quick glances, and perpetual multitasking. Yet the things that matter most—meaningful relationships, focused work, reflective thought—demand precisely the opposite: sustained attention, emotional presence, and the willingness to engage without immediate payoff. Choosing depth in such a world is not simply a preference—it is a form of resistance, and increasingly, a form of wisdom.

Depth is not merely a matter of effort or intellect; it is a function of *attention over time.* This principle holds across domains. In conversation, depth arises when we stay long enough with another person to move past the expected into the unsaid. In work, it emerges when we resist the temptation to switch tasks, allowing ideas to develop past the point of friction. In solitude, it appears when we stop reaching for distraction and begin listening to what surfaces in silence. None of these states are optimised by our current tools or norms. In fact, the default design of most digital platforms is structured to *prevent* this kind of engagement—breaking time into alerts, segmenting thought into notifications, and scattering presence across multiple threads at once.

Consider how this manifests in relationships. The quality of a conversation is directly related to the depth of attention we bring to it. Yet many of us now approach even our closest connections with divided awareness. We listen while scanning a device, reply while glancing at incoming messages, nod while mentally composing a post. This is not deliberate neglect—it is ambient dilution. The mere possibility of interruption reshapes the interaction. Research from communication scholars such as Sherry Turkle and Jenny Radesky shows that people report feeling less heard and less emotionally supported when a phone is visible during conversation—even if it remains untouched. Presence, it turns out, is not just a matter of behaviour but of *attentional posture.*

The same dilution occurs in work. Cal Newport has argued persuasively that the most valuable and satisfying cognitive tasks—what he terms "deep work"—require long periods of undistracted concentration. Yet in many professional environments, busyness is prized over focus. The open-plan office, the constant ping of collaboration tools, the culture of instant responsiveness all conspire against depth. Workers switch tasks on average every three minutes, and studies have shown that it can take upwards of twenty minutes to regain full concentration after an interruption. The result is a culture of fractured productivity: many things started, few completed with clarity or care.

But perhaps the most insidious casualty of shallow engagement is our relationship with ourselves. In the rare moments when external demands pause—waiting in line, walking alone, lying awake at night—we are conditioned to reach for stimulation rather than introspection. This reflex is not trivial. Boredom, historically, has been a fertile space for imagination, problem-solving, and emotional processing. It is the mind's invitation to wander freely and settle into something deeper. When we habitually avoid boredom through micro-stimulation—scrolling, swiping, tapping—we rob ourselves of the conditions necessary for inner depth. We remain occupied, but unrooted.

Choosing depth, then, requires conscious reorientation. It begins with recognising that attention is not just a cognitive resource—it is an ethical one. How we allocate it reflects what we value, and over time, *shapes who we become.* To cultivate depth is to protect that allocation, to create boundaries that allow focus to accumulate rather than dissipate. This is not simply a matter of time management, but of *attentional architecture.* The environment must be designed to support the kind of presence we wish to sustain.

This can take many forms. In relationships, it may mean instituting device-free meals or intentionally scheduling uninterrupted time with loved ones. In professional life, it may involve blocking out hours for deep focus, disabling non-essential notifications, or redesigning workspace layout to minimise distraction. In personal routines, it may mean establishing rituals of digital stillness: morning reading, evening walks, analogue hobbies. These practices are not nostalgic retreats—they are strategic structures. They reintroduce friction where the default has become frictionless. And in doing so, they create the conditions where depth can emerge.

Crucially, depth is not incompatible with digital life. It simply requires that we distinguish between tools and environments. A messaging app can facilitate connection, or it can fragment it. A browser can open a portal to focused learning, or it can diffuse curiosity across thirty tabs. The key is not abstinence, but *intentionality*. The tools themselves are neutral; the context in which we use them is not. By being deliberate about *how* and *when* we engage, we can repurpose even the most attention-fraying technologies toward more reflective ends.

There is also a psychological shift required—a willingness to stay with discomfort. Depth often begins in resistance: the awkward pause in conversation, the tedium of a blank page, the restlessness of unstructured time. These are the thresholds we tend to escape. But they are also the entry points to something richer. Staying put—to listen more fully, think more carefully, feel more deeply—is a kind of training. It builds the cognitive and emotional muscle necessary to live with complexity. And complexity, more than cleverness or speed, is what depth ultimately requires.

This cultivation is especially vital in a culture that increasingly mistakes *exposure* for *understanding*. Just because we see more does not mean we know more. A constant stream of headlines, posts, and data points creates the illusion of insight while reducing our capacity for analysis. We are informed but not integrated. True comprehension demands sustained engagement with a topic, repeated exposure, reflection, and synthesis. It asks us to slow down long enough for information to become knowledge—and knowledge to become wisdom. Without this slowing, we risk becoming consumers of content, not students of it.

The same principle applies to emotion. We encounter a tragedy online, feel a flash of outrage or empathy, perhaps share a post—and then scroll on. But depth in feeling, like depth in thought, takes time. It requires the space to sit with grief, to work through discomfort, to metabolise complexity. When our emotional responses are flattened into reactions and performed for visibility, we short-circuit the very processes that help us grow.

To choose depth is not to reject modern life—it is to live it more fully. It is to resist the cultural momentum that pushes us toward speed and surface, and to reclaim the quiet, sustained attention that allows meaning to take root. This does not require radical change, but consistent choice: fewer interruptions, longer pauses, better boundaries. Over time, these choices compound. They create a life not just of efficiency or engagement, but of coherence.

In a world that offers constant novelty, depth can feel inefficient. It is slow, sometimes invisible, and often unmeasurable. But it is also what nourishes us. It is where relationships flourish, where work becomes meaningful, and where the self comes into clearer view. The shallow world will not disappear. But it does not have to define us. We can still choose to go deeper—with our attention, our time, and our presence. Not because it is easy. But because it is essential.

# Chapter 3
# The New Architecture of Addiction

Addiction today rarely arrives in a bottle or a pill; it pings in your pocket, scrolls beneath your thumb, and pulses through likes, streaks, followers, and alerts. This is not metaphorical—it is structural. Somewhere between behavioural science and interface engineering, the platforms that dominate our digital lives have shifted from neutral tools into environments designed to captivate, exploiting neurological tendencies to convert fleeting curiosity into enduring compulsion. The ecosystem they create is one not of information, but of extraction: attention becomes currency, and the user becomes commodity.

What marks this system is subtlety rather than force. The addiction is not imposed; it is engineered. Habit loops, feedback cycles, and reward dynamics shape behaviour invisibly. Colours, notification rhythms, interface flows, and algorithmic nudges operate beneath awareness, bypassing conscious choice. Rarely do we decide to check our phones a hundred times a day. And yet we do. Each swipe and scroll deepens neural pathways that make this behaviour feel both automatic and necessary.

Neurology provides the foundation for this manipulation. Our brains are tuned to novelty and change—particularly social and emotional cues—because in ancestral contexts, they signalled opportunity or threat. Digital platforms weaponise this instinct using intermittent reinforcement and variable rewards, tools once confined to psychology labs, now woven into the architecture of daily screen life.

Consider the dopamine surge triggered by social notifications. Misunderstood as a chemical of pleasure, dopamine is more accurately a signal of anticipation. It drives seeking rather than enjoyment. When an app delivers a ping at unpredictable intervals, it activates this seeking system. Craving the resolution of uncertainty—who messaged, who reacted—becomes reinforcing. Over time, anticipation outstrips content as the source of satisfaction. This is no behavioural anomaly; it is deliberate design, known to engineers and product managers alike. Many users sense the cycle yet find it hard to escape.

The problem extends beyond persuasiveness; it is pervasiveness. Traditional addictions demanded proximity—a casino, a pub, a slot machine. Now they fit in the palm, cloaked as productivity, connection, even necessity. Email, messaging apps, calendars, team dashboards—they are indispensable yet complicit in entrenching compulsive habits. Tools and dependencies entwine. This is not convenience; it is entanglement.

Increasingly, the digital world functions as environment rather than tool. Interfaces, notifications, and engineered delays condition habits to serve platforms rather than users. Netflix autoplays episodes; TikTok continues the feed unprompted; social platforms manipulate suspense loops. These are behavioural scaffolds—designed to extend sessions, increase return visits, and convert time into monetisable data. The interface ceases to be neutral, subtly shaping cognition even while we believe we are in control.

Notifications illustrate this dynamic vividly. Ostensibly convenient, they operate as micro-hijacks—fracturing attention and training the brain to respond to external cues rather than internal priorities. Over time, hyper-reactivity develops; a device twitches, and so do we. Conscious intent is replaced by conditioned impulse. Opening an app for a quick check may result in forty-five minutes lost in streams of content, all without friction or reflection.

The consequences of this seamless design are not benign. Cognitive sovereignty erodes. Wants blur into habits; desires merge with defaults. Patience, focus, solitude—the very skills underpinning autonomy—atrophy. This is not accidental; it is systemically induced. Frictionless digital life produces a frayed internal world.

Ethics enter the picture here. When does persuasive design cross into exploitation? Claims of good intent—"we designed this to engage users"—cannot excuse outcomes. When features consistently foster compulsive behaviour, fatigue, or diminished wellbeing, the design itself must be interrogated.

Scholars now advocate ethical design incorporating digital friction. Small interventions—pauses, reminders, micro-prompts—reintroduce choice into systems optimised for impulse. These nudges shift behaviour from automatic to considered, restoring space for reflection.

Responsibility, of course, is shared. Users must interrogate the systems they inhabit, recognising not only what is offered, but how behaviour is shaped. This is not paranoia; it is perceptiveness. Addiction thrives in opacity; naming its techniques and experimenting with resistance recovers agency.

The architecture of modern addiction touches our mornings, evenings, workflows, and relationships. Understanding it is not merely critique—it is reclamation. The aim is not to demonise technology or romanticise the analogue, but to map an environment we cannot escape, and to navigate it deliberately. Awareness becomes our first defence. Where behaviour is engineered, resistance must be intentionally designed. What is required now is architecture that respects attention, enables reflection, restores boundaries, and preserves space—for silence, depth, and the unmediated self.

## Habit Loops and Feedback Hooks

When a person checks their phone without thinking—while waiting at a red light, standing in a lift, or queuing for coffee—it's rarely because of conscious intent. More often, it's the expression of an invisible pattern, triggered by context and executed automatically. This is the architecture of a habit loop at work. And in the digital age, it's not simply a by-product of convenience—it's a manufactured outcome. Technology companies have spent years refining the subtle art of behavioural design, embedding psychological triggers and neurological hooks into everyday interactions. The goal is simple but profound: *to turn engagement into instinct.*

At the heart of this lies a deceptively elegant model from behavioural psychology: the habit loop. Coined and popularised in part by

Charles Duhigg, the loop consists of three core components—cue, routine, and reward. A cue is a trigger that initiates the behaviour; the routine is the action itself; and the reward is the payoff that reinforces repetition. While this sequence was originally used to understand habits like smoking or nail-biting, it is now the foundational blueprint for app design, notification systems, and virtually every consumer-facing platform on the internet.

The most sophisticated systems don't just accommodate this loop—they *orchestrate it.* Consider Instagram. The cue might be a moment of boredom or a notification ping. The routine is the scrolling of the feed, watching Stories, or swiping through Reels. The reward comes in the form of social validation (likes, views), novelty (fresh content), or a fleeting sense of belonging. Each loop strengthens the association between the trigger and the action, gradually shifting the behaviour from conscious to automatic. Over time, the loop doesn't just persist—it *deepens*, colonising more moments of downtime, curiosity, or emotional restlessness.

What makes these loops especially potent is their integration with what behavioural scientists call *variable rewards*. Unlike predictable reinforcement, variable rewards are inconsistent in timing or outcome. This unpredictability mirrors the psychology behind slot machines—a framework known to be one of the most addictive in human experience. Each time we check our phone, we might see something thrilling (a message from someone we admire), something mundane (a system notification), or nothing at all. This uncertainty fuels repeated checking because our brain's reward system, particularly its dopaminergic pathways, becomes hypersensitive to the possibility of novelty. We're not addicted to the content—we're addicted to the *potential* of reward.

This is a critical distinction, and one that shifts the conversation away from morality and willpower toward mechanism and design. People are not failing to exercise self-control; they are responding predictably to environments engineered for compulsivity. A user's attention is not being lost—it's being *captured.* And what's being mistaken for distraction is, in fact, a predictable loop of stimulus and response. The more emotionally vulnerable we are—lonely, anxious, bored—the more likely these loops are to fire. It is a model of behaviour that thrives on emotional ambivalence and cognitive downtime.

The most successful digital platforms are those that have mastered the art of the *feedback hook*. A term popularised by Nir Eyal, the feedback hook is an extension of the habit loop—it not only drives repeated use but also draws the user into a cycle of *investment.* Each time a user creates content, adjusts settings, adds contacts, or interacts with others, they leave behind digital residue—data that customises their experience and subtly escalates their commitment. The more a person contributes, the harder it becomes to leave. This is not simply psychological inertia; it is behavioural tethering. Our digital habits are not just reinforced—they are *enmeshed* with our identity.

Crucially, the neurological basis for this is well established. The basal ganglia, a region of the brain involved in habit formation, automates repeated behaviours once they're sufficiently rehearsed. Meanwhile, the prefrontal cortex—responsible for decision-making and long-term planning—takes a back seat. This means that once a habit loop is ingrained, it operates below the level of deliberate intention. We don't *choose* to refresh our email for the sixth time in ten minutes; our brains have outsourced the behaviour to an autopilot system that privileges familiarity over logic.

This outsourcing has consequences—not just for our productivity, but for our sense of agency. When behaviours become automatic, they escape scrutiny. And when platforms are designed to exploit these loops, they shift us from users to subjects—participants in a behavioural experiment we never agreed to. It is here that the ethics of design come into sharp relief. What does it mean for a product to be "engaging" when its engagement strategy relies on neurological exploitation? At what point does clever design cross the line into manipulation?

This is not merely a philosophical question. It is a practical one, with direct implications for wellbeing, attention, and freedom. As research from Stanford's Persuasive Technology Lab and other institutions has shown, the integration of habit-forming mechanisms into app design increases usage time, but also correlates with spikes in stress, sleep disruption, and attentional fragmentation. What begins as convenience ends in compulsion. What begins as delight becomes dependence.

And this dependence is not evenly distributed. Younger users—whose neural circuits are still developing—are particularly susceptible to these loops. The habit loop becomes a developmental pathway, shaping not just behaviour but identity. A teenager who checks Snapchat 80 times a day is not making 80 separate decisions; they are running a loop 80 times—each time reinforcing a behavioural groove that bypasses self-reflection. The brain learns what it repeats, and in this case, it is learning *to need stimulation to feel normal.*

To address this challenge, we need more than awareness—we need *intervention.* But effective intervention begins with understanding. Understanding that our worst tech habits are not moral failings but neurobehavioural feedback loops. Understanding that resisting them is not simply about discipline but about *interrupting the sequence*—identifying the cue, altering the routine, and rethinking the reward. This is not a one-size-fits-all strategy; it requires experimentation, reflection, and environmental redesign.

For instance, removing cues—such as disabling push notifications—can weaken the loop by eliminating the trigger. Replacing routines—such as substituting a walk or a phone call for compulsive app checking—redirects behaviour while preserving emotional needs. And re-evaluating rewards—by asking whether the outcome actually nourishes or merely numbs—restores conscious agency to a formerly unconscious act. These are not trivial steps; they are behavioural rewrites. And like all rewrites, they take time, but offer durability.

Designers, too, have a role to play. Imagine systems that *discourage overuse*—apps that require a pause before scrolling resumes, platforms that surface long-term usage patterns, or features that make habit loops *visible* rather than invisible. Ethical design means recognising that when you shape attention, you shape lives—and doing so with care, transparency, and restraint.

At its core, the discussion of habit loops and feedback hooks is a discussion about *freedom*—the freedom to act with intention rather than impulse, to choose your inputs rather than be shaped by them. Our devices are not neutral tools; they are persuasive systems. And if we don't learn to read their cues, we risk becoming fluent only in reaction. Understanding habit loops isn't just psychological literacy—it is modern survival. It is the difference between being nudged and being moved. Between engaging with technology, and being consumed by it. Between using a tool, and becoming its extension.

## The Dopamine Design Model

There is a reason why the same person who struggles to focus on a book can spend hours tapping through TikTok videos. It isn't a matter of laziness, nor a flaw in willpower. It's the consequence of a system expertly engineered to stimulate the brain's reward circuits—again and again—without ever fully satisfying them. At the heart of this system lies dopamine: a neurotransmitter long misunderstood as a signal of pleasure, but in reality far more potent as a signal of *anticipation.* The digital world exploits this neurobiological quirk not through accident or excess, but by design. This is the dopamine design model: a behavioural architecture built to manipulate reward pathways for maximum engagement.

Dopamine does not flood the brain when we receive a reward—it spikes in expectation of a reward. This distinction is critical. What keeps us clicking, scrolling, or swiping isn't the certainty of gratification, but the *possibility* of it. The brain becomes a prediction engine, fixated on what might come next. And in environments where outcomes are inconsistent—where rewards are *intermittent*—dopamine surges are especially pronounced. This is known as *variable reinforcement*, and it is among the most reliable mechanisms for driving compulsive behaviour ever discovered.

Psychologists first studied this pattern in the 1950s through the work of B.F. Skinner. In a now-famous experiment, Skinner placed rats in boxes where pressing a lever would sometimes dispense a food pellet. When the reward was unpredictable, the rats pressed more frequently, more urgently, and for longer durations than when the reward was consistent. Intermittent reinforcement made the behaviour *resilient*—difficult to extinguish even when the reward disappeared altogether. This same dynamic now fuels much of our digital environment. The "pull-to-refresh" mechanism in social media apps mimics the lever in Skinner's box, while likes, mentions, and algorithmic feeds deliver just enough novelty to keep the brain hooked.

Instagram, Twitter, YouTube, and virtually every game or app that relies on habitual use incorporates elements of variable reinforcement. Users do not know whether the next refresh will reveal something trivial or something thrilling. Sometimes they are ignored, other times they are showered with social validation. It's the not-knowing—the gap between expectation and outcome—that creates what neuroscientists call a "reward prediction error," a key trigger of dopamine release. Importantly, dopamine is not a reward in itself. It's an attention allocator: it prioritises behaviours likely to lead to future rewards. The more frequently those prediction errors occur, the more sensitised the system becomes.

This is where gamification enters the equation. Gamification—the use of game-like mechanics in non-game settings—is not inherently manipulative. Used well, it can motivate learning, build positive habits, and increase engagement with otherwise tedious tasks. But in the wrong hands, it becomes a Trojan horse for compulsion. Points, streaks, badges, levels, and leaderboards provide a steady stream of artificial achievements. They offer quick hits of progress divorced from meaning or mastery. The user feels active, but the action is hollow. The satisfaction is shallow, and quickly replaced by the need for another fix. *Gamified environments reward participation without necessarily rewarding substance.*

Take Snapchat's "streaks" feature as an example. The mechanic is simple: send a message to a friend each day and maintain a running count of consecutive days. Break the streak, and it resets to zero. The feature provides no intrinsic value beyond a number on a screen, yet it compels millions of users to open the app daily—even if only to send an emoji or a blank message. It's a behavioural tether, designed to activate anticipation and prevent disconnection. The reward is not emotional depth or meaningful exchange—it's the avoidance of loss and the preservation of a metric.

Over time, the neurological consequence of this constant stimulation is what researchers call *hedonic adaptation.* The more frequently the brain is exposed to quick rewards, the more it recalibrates its expectations. Baseline satisfaction diminishes. The same stimulus no longer delivers the same hit. This is not unlike tolerance in substance use: more is needed to achieve the same effect. In the digital context, this manifests as rising screen time, lower attention spans, and a diminished capacity to derive joy from slower, subtler activities—such as reading a book, holding a conversation, or simply doing nothing.

Crucially, dopamine-driven design doesn't just affect *how much* we use technology—it changes *how we relate* to time, effort, and meaning. The constant availability of stimulation trains the brain to expect immediate payoff. If an app or website doesn't reward us within seconds, we abandon it. If a task requires sustained focus before yielding satisfaction, we avoid it. This is not a question of preference—it is a neurological adjustment. The environment shapes the brain, and the brain reshapes the self.

What's often overlooked in public discourse is that these design features are neither inevitable nor incidental. They are the product of deliberate choice. Entire teams within tech companies—behavioural scientists, user experience designers, data scientists—collaborate to fine-tune frictionless, addictive experiences. Their key performance indicators are metrics like time-on-site, retention, daily active users—not wellbeing, understanding, or depth. The business model rewards stickiness, and dopamine is the glue.

This raises unavoidable ethical questions. Should engineers be held accountable for the effects of the systems they build? Should the use of variable rewards be subject to regulation in the same way as gambling? Should children be exposed to gamified platforms that leverage cognitive vulnerabilities for commercial gain? These questions do not have easy answers, but avoiding them ensures one thing: that design will continue to prioritise engagement over agency.

One promising concept in response to this trend is *digital friction.* Unlike traditional design goals that aim to eliminate all obstacles to engagement, digital friction introduces intentional pauses, speed bumps, or constraints. These might include features like timed locks, focus modes, delayed notifications, or even prompts that require users to reflect before posting. By slowing down the loop between action and reward, friction reintroduces deliberation where impulse once reigned. It is not punitive—it is protective. *Friction is not failure; it is a boundary against exploitation.*

For users seeking to navigate this terrain more consciously, the first step is *awareness.* Once you understand how dopamine-driven loops work, you can begin to notice them in real-time. You can ask: Why am I reaching for my phone? What do I expect to find? Is this urge about connection—or stimulation? These questions interrupt the automaticity of the loop and make space for agency. Over time, that awareness can be paired with design choices—both technological and environmental—that recalibrate your reward system.

You might disable app notifications, move compulsive apps off your home screen, or set usage limits. You might replace streaks with intentions—asking not how many days in a row you've logged into an app, but how many days you've spent your time intentionally. You might rebuild your attention span not through grand acts of discipline, but through small experiments in stillness. The goal is not abstinence from technology, but sovereignty over it.

Ultimately, the dopamine design model reveals a troubling truth: that in many digital environments, *you are not the customer—you are the product.* Your attention is monetised, your behaviour is shaped, and your neurochemistry is the terrain of design. But knowledge is power. And when you understand the systems shaping your urges, you are no longer just a user—you become a designer of your own attention.

This is not a rejection of pleasure, novelty, or even gamification. It is a reassertion of depth, intention, and freedom in an age that profits from their erosion. The dopamine system is not your enemy—it is your compass. But like any compass, it must be calibrated, or it will always point to whatever pings the loudest. Recalibration begins with recognition. And recognition begins here.

## Why Notifications Work So Well

A single ping can fracture an entire hour of deep work. A vibration on the wrist can override a conversation, derail a thought, or reorient attention before the recipient even knows what the alert contains. This is not a matter of weakness or lack of discipline. Notifications succeed not because we are careless, but because they are expertly crafted to bypass conscious decision-making and trigger fast, automatic responses. The brilliance of the notification lies in its subtlety. It is a micro-interruption—so brief as to seem harmless, yet powerful enough to hijack focus, prime anticipation, and invite compulsive checking. And it is no accident. *Notifications are not alerts—they are levers of behavioural control.*

What makes a notification so potent is that it collapses space between signal and response. The moment the alert sounds, our attentional system, governed by a complex network of neural circuits, is involuntarily engaged. The orienting response—first described by Ivan Pavlov and later formalised by neuroscientist Eugene Sokolov—is an ancient survival mechanism. When something in the environment suddenly changes, the brain reallocates cognitive resources toward identifying the potential threat or reward. This isn't optional. It's reflexive. The ping becomes the new centre of gravity.

In the digital context, the contents of the notification may be entirely mundane—a retweet, a calendar reminder, a low battery alert. But the brain doesn't wait for substance before reacting. It responds to *salience*, not significance. And developers understand this. That's why notifications are designed not merely to inform but to interrupt. The colour red is commonly used for badges because it conveys urgency. Haptic feedback (like a buzz on the wrist) exploits tactile channels that are harder to ignore. Sounds are carefully chosen for distinctiveness and novelty. The result is a system optimised to capture attention regardless of whether attention is warranted.

The psychological underpinning of this mechanism is reinforcement learning. When a notification occasionally delivers something rewarding—a message from a loved one, a work opportunity, a social endorsement—it triggers a dopamine spike. The brain encodes this as a valuable event. But crucially, the value is not in the reward itself—it's in the association between the alert and the *possibility* of reward. This intermittent reinforcement schedule mirrors the dynamic of slot machines: not every pull delivers a win, but the next one might. *Notifications turn the phone into a casino in your pocket.*

The consequences of this dynamic are measurable. Studies show that it takes an average of 23 minutes to regain full focus after an interruption. Even when users do not check the notification, the mere presence of a device—visible, nearby, and active—can reduce cognitive capacity, a phenomenon termed "brain drain." In experiments conducted at the University of Texas, participants who had their phones in another room performed significantly better on tasks requiring focus than those who had their phones face down on the table. *The potential for interruption is itself an attention tax.*

Furthermore, notifications destabilise temporal rhythms. Human concentration relies on cycles—ultradian rhythms of alertness and fatigue that govern how long we can sustain mental effort. Disrupting these rhythms with frequent, unsynchronised alerts fragments not only task engagement but also the mind's ability to settle into deeper, more reflective states. The effect is cumulative. What begins as a useful tool for reminders becomes a persistent architecture of interruption—one that reshapes the texture of experience and the quality of thought.

Critically, not all notifications are equal. Passive alerts—such as delivery confirmations or system updates—tend to be ignored without much disruption. But *social notifications*—those tied to identity, status, or relationships—trigger far stronger responses. A message from a friend, a mention on social media, a reaction to a post—these involve *social reward pathways* linked to oxytocin, serotonin, and endogenous opioids. They activate the same circuitry involved in feelings of connection, approval, and belonging. This is why turning off email alerts is easier than disabling Instagram notifications. The latter is not just about information; it's about self-perception.

Platforms know this. Notification algorithms are tuned not just to inform, but to maximise return visits. Facebook's notification system, for instance, once delayed notifications until it predicted the user was most likely to respond. Gmail's "priority inbox" and iOS's "scheduled summary" may seem like efforts to reduce noise, but they are still governed by engagement heuristics. The goal is not neutrality—it's *relevance that drives action.* And the boundary between service and manipulation becomes blurrier with every iteration.

There is also a phenomenon known as *phantom vibration syndrome*—the false perception that one's phone is vibrating or ringing when it isn't. This isn't a hallucination, but a reflection of hypervigilance. The user has become so conditioned to anticipate notifications that the nervous system begins to simulate them. *The body learns to expect the interruption even when it doesn't arrive.* This speaks volumes about how deeply these micro-signals are embedded into our neural patterns. The notification is no longer an external cue—it becomes an internalised rhythm.

Some technologists argue that notifications are value-neutral. After all, they are settings that users can configure. But this perspective ignores the asymmetry of design power. Defaults matter. Most users do not customise notification settings, and developers know this. What ships as "on by default" becomes behavioural infrastructure. And even when controls are available, they often lack granularity. You can silence all alerts, but not just the trivial ones. You can enable "do not disturb," but at the cost of also muting potentially meaningful messages. The result is a design trade-off that favours either *always on* or *completely off*—rarely something considered and intentional.

There is, however, a growing movement toward *attention-aware design.* This includes features like notification batching, app-specific quiet hours, and modes that restrict alerts during deep work. Apple's "Focus Mode," Android's "Digital Wellbeing," and third-party tools like Forest or Freedom are nascent attempts to create friction around interruption. But they are workarounds, not foundations. *The architecture of the attention economy still depends on the notification as its primary gateway to engagement.*

To reclaim agency, the user must reverse engineer the logic of notification design. Begin by mapping your alert triggers. Which ones are time-sensitive? Which ones are merely habitual? Disable the latter. Separate utility from addiction. Introduce delay—by scheduling time to check messages rather than responding instantly. Reduce ambiguity—by grouping alerts into categories of relevance. Shift the locus of control from app to user. Every reduction in ambient interruption creates space for sustained thought.

Perhaps the most radical move is also the most modest: *treat your attention as if it matters.* Because it does. Notifications are not neutral pings. They are calls for your time, your energy, your mental clarity. And while the device may be engineered for interruption, the human mind is wired for focus. To guard that focus is not a retreat from modernity—it is a demand for sovereignty in the face of design that too often assumes compliance.

Why do notifications work so well? Because they are the digital equivalent of a tap on the shoulder—at the exact moment your guard is down. But when you know how the system works, you can turn that tap into a pause. You can look before reacting. And sometimes, you can choose not to turn around at all.

## When Neutral Design Becomes Manipulation

There is a quiet fiction at the heart of modern technology—that design is neutral. That interfaces merely present options, that menus simply organise possibilities, that clicks and swipes are voluntary choices in an open field of agency. But when a child taps "Skip Ads" five hundred times before breakfast, or when a late-night scroll morphs into an unplanned purchase, or when users repeatedly forget how they arrived at a screen they didn't intend to open, it becomes clear: *what we call "choice" is often a carefully shaped path.* And that path is paved not with neutrality but with intention—intention engineered by others.

To understand where neutrality ends and manipulation begins, one must start with the concept of *choice architecture*. Coined by behavioural economists Richard Thaler and Cass Sunstein, the term refers to the way in which decisions are influenced by how options are presented. In theory, this applies to everything from organ donation defaults to cafeteria layouts. In practice, it now applies most pervasively to apps, platforms, and digital ecosystems—environments designed not to display information, but to shape user action. *Every scroll depth, autoplay delay, and frictionless login is a behavioural nudge masquerading as interface design.*

The ethical problem is not that nudges exist—they always have. Architects nudge people to take stairs by placing them centrally. Supermarkets nudge buyers by positioning impulse items at eye level. But what makes digital design uniquely potent is the scale, speed, and granularity with which it can adapt in real time. Unlike a physical shelf, a digital interface learns. It A/B tests. It personalises. It optimises not for human flourishing, but for retention, click-through, and engagement. The feedback loop is tighter, the data is richer, and the goal is often less about utility than about compulsion.

This is where design crosses a threshold. What begins as user-centric becomes user-exploitative. The frictionless experience—the sacred grail of modern UX—becomes a slippery slope toward mindless engagement. Take infinite scroll, first introduced by Aza Raskin, who later came to regret the invention. Designed to eliminate the need for pagination, it subtly removed the natural stopping cues that help users reflect or disengage. *What used to be a page now has no end. And what used to be a decision now becomes default behaviour.*

Or consider autoplay. Ostensibly a convenience feature, it removes the need to press play. But functionally, it removes the opportunity to stop. Streaming platforms that queue the next episode in five seconds are not helping users save time—they are helping platforms claim it. This logic extends to notification design, algorithmic timelines, even the placement of "accept all" buttons on cookie banners. When every interface is designed to maximise time-on-platform, neutrality becomes a myth.

The ethical tension lies in the *intentional asymmetry*. Designers and engineers hold far more knowledge about the user than the user holds about the system. They know which button placements yield higher conversions. They know what time of day you're most likely to respond to a nudge. They know which colours evoke urgency and which phrases increase compliance. This is not merely predictive—it is prescriptive. *The interface is not just guiding behaviour; it is scripting it.*

And unlike traditional advertising, which is visible and recognisable as persuasion, manipulative design embeds influence invisibly into the fabric of interaction. There is no warning label on the infinite scroll. No disclosure on the dopamine curve baked into social notifications. No opt-out for "recommended for you" feeds that learn to addict you better with every click. The very features that are most manipulative are those that present themselves as harmless, helpful, or even user-friendly. This is what makes them so effective—and so difficult to resist.

Resistance, however, is not futile. It just requires reframing what resistance looks like. The dominant metaphor in tech culture has long been *frictionlessness*—the idea that the best experience is the one with the fewest barriers. But as researchers such as Tristan Harris and James Williams have pointed out, *not all friction is bad.* In fact, *digital friction*—the deliberate reintroduction of time, effort, or reflection into design—can serve as a crucial counterweight to manipulation.

Friction can be as simple as a confirmation step before posting. A delay before a message can be sent. A prompt that asks, "Are you sure you want to open this app again?" Friction slows the automatic and invites the intentional. It restores a sliver of deliberation into otherwise reflexive action. Gmail's "Undo Send" option is not just a feature—it is a moment of grace. Apple's "Screen Time" weekly report is not merely data—it is a mirror. These moments, small as they are, return the user to the centre of their own experience.

There is also an argument to be made for *designing for dignity*—a concept that goes beyond utility or usability. Dignity-centred design assumes that users are not just attention resources but moral agents. It respects their autonomy, not by offering endless options, but by offering meaningful ones. It avoids dark patterns—deceptive interface tactics like hidden fees, misdirection, or disguised opt-outs—that treat manipulation as a feature, not a flaw. And it embraces transparency: showing how recommendations are made, why alerts are triggered, and how data is used.

Of course, some might argue that users are ultimately responsible. That they can turn off notifications, delete apps, install blockers, or simply exercise more self-control. But this argument presumes that design is passive, and that users have infinite willpower. *It ignores the reality that choice is never made in a vacuum—it is always shaped by environment.* The same user who ignores an alert at noon may respond to it at midnight. The same interface that feels neutral in isolation may become manipulative in context.

This is not a plea for regulation—though regulation may have a role. It is a call for awareness. For designers to confront the ethical weight of their choices. For platforms to measure success not just in engagement metrics but in human outcomes. And for users to begin seeing design not as background noise but as active influence.

When neutral design becomes manipulation, the responsibility shifts. Not solely to the individual, but to the creators who wield disproportionate power. And with that power comes a question that cannot be deferred: *What kind of attention does this design produce? What kind of behaviour does it reward? And what kind of person does it assume the user is becoming?*

The answers to these questions are not abstract. They are built into every menu layout, every swipe animation, every loading bar. Design is destiny—but only if we stop noticing. If instead we build friction into our tools, intention into our clicks, and ethics into our code, we can begin to reclaim the digital space as something more than a mirror of exploitation. We can make it a space of agency, awareness, and alignment.

Because in the end, design is never neutral. It either helps us act on our values—or it helps us forget we had them.

# Chapter 4
# The Cost of Fragmented Focus

There is a cost to living in a world engineered for constant interruption, and it is rarely obvious at first glance. It is not tallied in hours spent online, notifications received, or tabs left open in your browser. The true price is paid in attention—specifically, in our growing inability to sustain it. Beneath the surface of our screen-saturated lives, what erodes is not only productivity but the very capacity to think clearly, to remember accurately, to engage fully. We are not simply distracted; we are being trained to be distractible.

For centuries, attention was regarded as a virtue—an indicator of discipline, presence, even intelligence. Philosophers from Aristotle to William James treated it as an act of the will, a gatekeeper of perception and meaning. Today, attention is no longer protected; it is harvested, fragmented, and redistributed across a landscape meticulously designed for interruption. Our devices do not merely invite focus—they compete for it, relentlessly and without pause.

Consider the cognitive switching penalty, a phenomenon long studied in laboratory settings but now visible in daily life. Rapidly moving between tasks—replying to messages mid-meeting, toggling between spreadsheets and newsfeeds—comes at a measurable mental cost. Accuracy drops, working memory falters, reaction time slows. Yet this depletion rarely registers consciously; instead, we misinterpret it as restlessness or boredom, prompting yet another switch. The more we flit, the more we fragment ourselves, and the more we mistake motion for productivity.

This illusion feeds directly into the myth of multitasking, long heralded as a mark of competence. Neuroscience paints a different picture: humans do not multitask; we toggle. The brain cannot truly attend to multiple cognitively demanding tasks at once. What we call multitasking is rapid serial task-switching, with each transition exacting its own toll. Knowledge workers who check email dozens of times a day compound these costs, splintering attention into shards too small to think with. The result is a culture of chronic partial attention, where nothing—neither work, nor conversation, nor reflection—receives our full cognitive presence.

The implications stretch deeper. Attention is not merely a tool for productivity; it is a prerequisite for reflection. When attention is shallow, thought becomes shallow. Research links screen-mediated behaviour with reduced capacity for deep reading—the kind of engagement that develops critical reasoning. Habitual scrolling and skimming cultivate speed at the expense of comprehension. We become fluent in scanning but less fluent in understanding.

Memory, too, suffers. Focused attention, working memory, and long-term encoding form a delicate chain. Interruptions—pings, scrolls, new tabs—break that chain, preventing memory from forming. This helps explain the sense of busy emptiness digital environments often leave behind: we are constantly active but rarely present. Even when recalling a video, article, or conversation, we struggle, because the brain cannot retain what was never fully attended to.

Technology is not neutral. Just as the printing press shaped cognition by privileging linear argument, the screen privileges immediacy, reactivity, and fragmentation. Frequent exposure to digital media fosters a cognitive style that is fast, shallow, and externally cued. Our thoughts become reactive rather than reflective; our opinions more rigid, less nuanced; our conversations shorter, louder, more performative. In losing attention, we lose the mental habits that sustain depth.

The consequences are social as well as individual. In a culture where distraction is normal, attentiveness itself is devalued. In meetings, classrooms, and families, sustained focus is rare—and sometimes even suspect. We glorify busyness, dismiss presence, and in doing so, hollow out experiences that require undivided attention: relationships, learning, creativity, contemplation. These pursuits demand not merely time, but uninterrupted time.

Meanwhile, the business logic of digital platforms actively undermines focus. Attention is a commodity; fragmentation drives profit. Every interruption generates data, every click produces revenue. A fundamental misalignment emerges: the brain craves coherence, the market profits from disruption. Without recognising this tension, we continue outsourcing our attentional agency to systems that care nothing for our interests.

Reclaiming that agency demands more than discipline; it requires structural insight. We must understand how attention is fragmented—not only by sheer volume, but by design. We must interrogate the stories we tell ourselves about productivity, multitasking, and the value of constant availability. We must notice when a glance becomes a loop, a check becomes an hour lost, a thought is truncated by an alert. We must notice that we are no longer noticing.

In the chapters ahead, these dynamics will be explored with rigor. You will encounter the science of cognitive switching costs and the brain's response to interruption. You will see how so-called multitasking diminishes not only output but insight. You will examine how attention, memory, and reasoning are reshaped by technologies engineered for speed and scale. And you will begin to reclaim what it means to focus in a world that profits from distraction.

Attention is more than a resource; it is a mode of being. Guard it, and you preserve not just your time, but the very conditions of thought. Neglect it, and you forfeit more than hours—you forfeit the depth and clarity that make life intelligible and meaningful.

## Cognitive Switching Penalty

A human brain, though astonishing in its complexity, was not built for rapid transitions between competing tasks. Yet this is exactly how most people now work, live, and interact with the digital world. The average professional shifts attention more than 1,100 times per day, toggling between tabs, threads, platforms, messages, and tasks with near-constant frequency. But this modern style of engagement is not without cognitive cost. What feels like quick adaptation is, in fact, a series of invisible losses—of time, of focus, and of mental energy. *The more frequently we switch, the less efficiently we think.*

The phenomenon at the centre of this dynamic is known as the **cognitive switching penalty**. Unlike a physical tax that announces itself loudly, this penalty is quiet and cumulative. Every time we redirect our attention from one cognitive task to another, even momentarily, the brain must adjust. Neural resources are reallocated, working memory is partially flushed, and contextual cues are discarded. These micro-transitions consume measurable amounts of mental energy and time—often more than we realise. Studies conducted by the American Psychological Association and Stanford University have shown that even brief interruptions—such as glancing at a phone notification—can double error rates and significantly slow the completion of complex tasks. More subtly, they degrade the *quality* of thought, replacing nuance and depth with hurried skimming and reactive output.

The term "task-switching" may sound benign, but its real-world implications are stark. Consider the structure of focused thought. To write a clear argument, solve a mathematical problem, plan a strategic decision, or process a complex interpersonal conversation requires a stable mental workspace—a kind of cognitive continuity. When this continuity is interrupted by an alert, an open inbox, or an impulsive web search, the mind is forced to shift context. And unlike a computer, which can suspend and resume programs with seamless precision, the human brain incurs what researchers call *resumption lag*—the time it takes to remember where you were, what you were doing, and why it mattered.

This resumption lag is not just theoretical. In experimental settings, participants asked to complete high-cognitive-load tasks while being interrupted took on average 50% longer and committed up to twice as many mistakes compared to those allowed to work without disruption. But beyond the metrics, there is an existential dimension: *distraction erodes not just performance, but a sense of self-mastery.* Repeated interruption undermines the feeling of completion and coherence, leaving many with a vague sense of mental clutter and dissatisfaction by day's end, even if they were busy the entire time.

Some argue that task-switching is an unavoidable feature of modern life—that to be effective is to be adaptive, responsive, and fluid. While there is truth in the need for agility, this rationale confuses responsiveness with fragmentation. *Responsiveness is deliberate; fragmentation is compulsive.* The former is strategic and time-bound. The latter is ambient, constant, and self-reinforcing. What makes the switching penalty particularly pernicious today is that many of its triggers are engineered to be irresistible. The red dot on an app icon, the subtle vibration in a pocket, the numerical badge tallying new alerts—these are not neutral signals. They are part of an attention economy that thrives on volatility, and they train us to prioritise the *new* over the *important*, the *urgent* over the *essential.*

And there is no neutrality in the tools we use. Consider the design of the modern smartphone. It is not built as a single-purpose tool for communication or productivity; it is a portal to dozens of competing attention streams, each vying to hijack cognitive priority. When one attempts to read a work email and receives a banner about a social media mention, the switch may feel trivial. But multiply that process over an hour, a day, a week—and the cumulative effects are profound. *What you think about shapes who you become—but only if you are allowed to stay with it long enough to do the shaping.*

The myth of the multitasker compounds the problem. Many professionals—particularly those in knowledge work—have internalised the idea that juggling tasks is not just a necessity, but a sign of competence. In reality, multitasking in the human brain is a misnomer. True cognitive multitasking, involving simultaneous attention to two complex tasks, is neurologically implausible for most people. What we call multitasking is, in fact, rapid task-switching, with attention ricocheting back and forth in a way that impairs both tasks. Imaging studies using fMRI have shown that during such switches, the brain actually enters a transitional state that is less efficient at both tasks, creating what researchers call *dual-task interference.* The illusion of progress hides real decline.

The switching penalty also extends beyond performance to emotional and relational consequences. When our attention is perpetually divided, we struggle to be fully present—not just with tasks, but with people. A conversation interrupted by phone glances becomes stilted. A moment of reflection lost to an email reply goes unfinished. This form of attentional drift creates a low-grade disconnection—not enough to alarm, but enough to accumulate. It fosters what social psychologists describe as *absentee presence*—being physically somewhere but mentally elsewhere. Over time, this frays not only productivity, but trust and intimacy.

One of the great ironies is that many of the behaviours that trigger the switching penalty are driven by a desire to be more efficient. We check messages quickly to "stay on top of things," answer emails mid-task to avoid backlog, or bounce between tabs to "make the most" of our time. But the science is unequivocal: *interrupted work takes longer, yields poorer results, and feels less satisfying*. The promise of multitasking is speed; the reality is cognitive disarray.

What, then, is the alternative? The solution is not nostalgia for a pre-digital world, but the deliberate cultivation of *monotasking*—single-task attention practiced with intention. This does not mean rigidly avoiding all interruptions, but creating time blocks for deep work, turning off non-essential notifications, and structuring environments that support sustained focus. It means reclaiming *attentional agency*—deciding where your mind goes, and keeping it there long enough for thinking to matter.

Crucially, monotasking is not about doing less. It is about doing better. It is the precondition for insight, creativity, and strategic clarity—capacities that cannot be summoned on command but must be *cultivated through continuity*. When the mind is allowed to stay with an idea, it can explore nuance, integrate knowledge, and synthesise complexity. These are the hallmarks of deep cognition, and they do not occur in fractured mental states.

None of this is to suggest that multitasking will—or should—disappear entirely. Some tasks *can* be interwoven with relative ease: walking while thinking, listening to a podcast while doing dishes. But the key distinction is between *mechanical combination* and *cognitive interference*. The former is benign. The latter is costly. And that cost must be recognised not as a flaw in personal discipline, but as a by-product of systems optimised for fragmentation.

Understanding the cognitive switching penalty is not simply about improving personal productivity. It is about acknowledging how attention—our most foundational cognitive resource—is being depleted by default. It is about asking better questions: What kind of work do we want to do? What kind of relationships do we want to sustain? What kind of thoughts do we wish to have the mental space to finish? These are not just logistical questions; they are philosophical ones.

Because when we lose the capacity for sustained attention, we do not merely lose time—we lose access to our own minds. And no device, no app, no platform will ever be worth that trade.

## The Myth of Multitasking

No concept has seduced the modern worker more thoroughly than the belief that multitasking is a virtue. The idea that one can simultaneously compose emails, attend meetings, monitor social media, and reply to messages—all while remaining intellectually sharp and emotionally available—has become both a cultural ideal and a professional expectation. But it is a fiction. *The science is clear: multitasking is not efficient, it is expensive.* Not financially, but cognitively.

What most people describe as multitasking is, in reality, task-switching. The brain does not perform two high-level tasks at once; it toggles between them, often within milliseconds, expending resources each time it shifts. The cost of this constant toggling includes reduced accuracy, slower processing, and greater mental fatigue. And while these effects are often subtle, their consequences are cumulative. A growing body of research, including studies from Stanford University and the University of Sussex, has shown that heavy multitaskers are more prone to distraction, have poorer memory retention, and exhibit diminished executive control—the very faculties needed for thoughtful work.

Still, the myth persists. Perhaps because multitasking *feels* productive. Typing during a video call or scrolling during a lecture can create the illusion of efficiency. But this is performance, not progress. Neuroimaging studies reveal that rather than splitting attention between two tasks, the brain actually suppresses one in order to activate another. In doing so, it incurs what researchers call a "switch cost"—a measurable dip in cognitive capacity that lingers for several minutes after each transition. *The more we switch, the less we retain. The more we juggle, the more we drop.*

Multitasking becomes especially costly when paired with digital media. The modern digital environment is designed to compete for attention with intensity and frequency. Background scrolling—checking feeds, browsing headlines, monitoring chat windows—may appear harmless, especially when done "passively," but even these micro-engagements draw down cognitive resources. The brain must parse visual stimuli, assess social cues, interpret emotional valence, and store data in working memory. That these actions happen quickly does not make them free. As psychologist Daniel Kahneman notes, attention is not just a mental act—it is an expenditure. And like any budget, overspending leads to depletion.

Nowhere is this more visible than in the context of learning and deep work. Whether reading, writing, or problem-solving, these activities depend on uninterrupted attention. Even a brief glance at a phone can interrupt the mental scaffolding required for comprehension. Researchers at the University of California, Irvine, found that after a typical workplace interruption, it takes over 23 minutes on average to return to the original task with full focus. Worse, the quality of the resumed work is usually poorer—more surface-level, less accurate, and more prone to error. *Multitasking reduces not just quantity, but quality.*

This is not only a productivity issue. It is a thinking issue. Philosophers have long noted that thought requires duration—what French philosopher Simone Weil called *attention as a form of prayer.* That is, deep thinking demands sustained presence. When thought is fractured by background scrolling or digital interruptions, it tends toward triviality. Instead of insights, we get impressions. Instead of synthesis, we get skimming. This erosion of mental depth has profound implications not only for individual cognition but for collective discourse. Shallow engagement breeds shallow culture.

The persistence of the multitasking myth is not simply a result of individual misunderstanding—it is structurally encouraged. Many workplace cultures reward availability over focus, responsiveness over reflection. Emails are expected to be answered promptly. Status indicators flash green to denote productivity. Workers feel pressure to always be "on," fearing that to disengage from peripheral streams is to fall behind. But this is a misreading of effectiveness. *Real productivity is not measured by volume of activity, but by quality of output.* And quality suffers when the mind is constantly split.

Education is another domain where the multitasking myth is quietly damaging. Students are often encouraged—or at least permitted—to browse supplementary materials, chat with peers, or consult digital resources while attending lectures or working on assignments. Yet empirical studies show that students who multitask during learning retain significantly less information and perform worse on comprehension tests. Moreover, the habit of dividing attention during intellectual tasks teaches the mind to expect stimulation, rather than to generate it. *The ability to stay with one thing—the essence of deep work—atrophies when it is never exercised.*

There is also a psychological cost. Chronic multitasking has been linked to increased stress, reduced satisfaction, and a diminished sense of agency. When attention is always divided, we begin to feel fragmented ourselves. This sense of being "spread thin" is not just metaphorical—it is neurobiological. The prefrontal cortex, responsible for planning, decision-making, and impulse control, becomes overtaxed, leading to reduced capacity for reflection, self-regulation, and long-term thinking. We move faster but understand less. We do more but remember less. We work harder but feel less fulfilled.

There are those who argue that multitasking is a necessary adaptation to the complexity of modern life. After all, the demands on our time and attention are unprecedented. But this line of reasoning ignores a critical distinction: adaptation is not the same as optimisation. The fact that we *can* divide attention does not mean we *should*. Nor does it mean we do it well. The goal is not to abandon all forms of digital multitasking—this would be neither realistic nor desirable—but to recognise its limitations and use it sparingly, not as a default mode.

Background scrolling deserves particular scrutiny. It is often justified as a harmless way to fill idle moments, reduce boredom, or stay informed. But what is rarely acknowledged is its opportunity cost.

Every scroll is a choice—not only about content, but about attention. And every background tab open during a task is a form of leakage, draining cognitive bandwidth that could be used for more meaningful or demanding thought. The cost of this leakage is rarely noticed in the moment. But over time, it accumulates, shaping not just how we work, but who we become.

The antidote to multitasking is not austerity, but intentionality. It is the deliberate practice of monotasking—focusing on one cognitively significant task at a time, without splitting attention across multiple streams. This requires both design and discipline: creating work environments that support focus, turning off unnecessary notifications, resisting the reflex to check devices during moments of boredom. It also involves cultural shifts: reframing availability not as virtue, but vulnerability; treating sustained attention as a scarce and precious asset.

There are practical steps that support this shift. Batch processing of emails, designated blocks for deep work, mindfulness practices to train attention, and the physical separation of tasks—all help mitigate the temptation to multitask. But beyond tactics, what is needed is a revaluation of focus itself. *We must come to see undivided attention not as a luxury, but as a foundation of clarity, creativity, and meaningful engagement.*

Multitasking, when mythologised, becomes a thief. It steals time without asking. It undermines focus without warning. And perhaps most damaging of all, it deceives us into thinking we are accomplishing more when we are, in fact, diminishing our cognitive potential. The promise of the multitasking mind is alluring—but the price is mental fragmentation. To think deeply, to understand fully, to live attentively—we must stop pretending that the mind is a machine optimised for parallel processing. It is not. It is a tool for depth. And that depth is only possible when we give it our full attention.

## Shorter Attention, Shallower Thinking

In 2004, researchers estimated the average human attention span to be around two and a half minutes. By 2012, it had fallen to seventy-five seconds. Today, on digital platforms, it is often measured in seconds—eight for YouTube videos, three before a user scrolls past a post, and less than one before switching browser tabs. This isn't a trivia fact—it's a window into the structural rewiring of the modern mind. *Attention is collapsing, and with it, the capacity for depth.* What once required deliberate effort—reading, reflecting, grappling with complexity—is now increasingly outsourced, truncated, or avoided altogether. We are not just spending time differently; we are *thinking* differently.

This erosion is not incidental. It is the product of design. Every swipe, ping, and autoplay feature on our screens is engineered to fragment attention. Platforms are built to interrupt, entice, and redirect. Their business model depends on it. The longer users stay, the more data is harvested and the more ads are served. But sustained presence—*real*, contemplative attention—is not profitable. It slows engagement, reduces refreshes, and lowers revenue. So instead, digital environments incentivise speed, novelty, and quantity of interaction over depth or continuity. *And what the environment rewards, the mind learns to replicate.*

This is not just about distraction. It is about *cognitive consequence*. The human brain is plastic—it reshapes itself in response to how it is used. If the bulk of daily attention is spent in rapid, shallow bursts, constantly scanning and shifting, then neural pathways associated with sustained focus and analytical reasoning weaken over time. Nicholas Carr, in *The Shallows*, articulates this concern with clarity: the medium through which we consume information shapes the kind of thinking we do. Skimming begets scanning. Endless scrolling begets impatience. Hyperlinking trains the mind to leap, not linger.

Empirical evidence supports this. A study conducted at the University of California, San Diego, found that digital multitaskers—those frequently engaged with multiple streams of media—performed worse on tests of working memory, attention control, and task persistence. Crucially, they also *overestimated* their ability to multitask, highlighting a kind of cognitive blindness. Other research at Microsoft found that office workers interrupted by emails or IMs took an average of fifteen minutes to regain serious mental focus, even if the interruption lasted seconds. Each ping not only severs the thought at hand—it *reshapes* the architecture of future thought.

Attention is more than focus. It is the gateway to meaning. Without sustained attention, the mind struggles to do the slow, recursive work of connecting ideas, building insight, or evaluating nuance. These capacities—essential to critical thinking, learning, and creativity—depend on uninterrupted stretches of time. Philosopher William James once wrote that the faculty of voluntarily bringing back a wandering attention over and over again is the *very root of judgment, character, and will.* Today, that faculty is under assault.

Part of the issue is definitional. Many conflate attention span with willpower, assuming it's a matter of discipline. But attention is not merely a character trait—it is a cognitive function shaped by environment, habits, and neurochemistry. The glut of stimuli on our screens creates a form of attentional hyperactivity: the mind, expecting interruption, pre-empts focus. This anticipation itself becomes a distraction. Just knowing a phone is nearby—even if turned off—can reduce cognitive performance, as demonstrated by a 2017 study from the University of Texas at Austin. The mind is not just distracted *by* technology; it becomes habituated *to* distraction.

More dangerously, this decline in attention correlates with a decline in *depth.* Depth of thought requires more than information retention. It demands *cognitive patience*—the willingness to stay with a complex idea, to entertain ambiguity, to mentally wrestle with contradiction or uncertainty. This is not merely an academic concern. In democratic societies, depth underpins deliberation. In relationships, it underpins empathy. In professions, it underpins problem-solving. Shallower attention erodes all three.

This isn't an indictment of technology, but of its unchecked design. Not all digital tools diminish attention. Long-form podcasts, for instance, have surged in popularity precisely because they provide narrative continuity in a sea of fragmentation. E-readers offer distraction-free environments for immersive reading. Meditation apps help train attentional control. The difference lies in *intent.* Tools designed to support cognitive engagement are scarce, while those engineered for compulsive consumption dominate.

Part of reclaiming attention involves interrogating the norms we've come to accept. That it's acceptable to reply to texts during dinner. That background TV or YouTube is an ordinary part of working. That rapid response times signal competence. These habits, while seemingly benign, chip away at our ability to *be present*—with others, with ideas, with ourselves. Presence is a precondition for insight. Without it, we default to surface understanding.

A further complication lies in how shortened attention alters our expectations of content itself. Articles are skimmed, not read. Books are summarised, not studied. Ideas are judged by headlines, not arguments. What doesn't grab immediately is dismissed. In such a climate, subtlety becomes a liability and complexity a burden. Yet *truth*, especially on difficult questions—whether scientific, moral, or political—rarely arrives in soundbites. It requires the kind of thinking that is now structurally discouraged.

To be clear, attention is not vanishing. It is being redistributed. People still concentrate deeply—on games, binge-worthy series, immersive fiction, niche obsessions. But the skill of applying *voluntary attention* to things that are initially hard or slow—dense reading, abstract thought, delayed gratification—is eroding. And this skill is not optional. It underpins our ability to learn, to reflect, to innovate.

The implications extend to education. Classrooms increasingly contend with the challenge of maintaining student focus in an environment of ambient digital distraction. Teachers report rising difficulty in getting students to complete assigned readings or engage in sustained discussions. Meanwhile, schools adopt digital platforms that often replicate the engagement metrics of social media—likes, badges, streaks—further encouraging short-term reward loops over long-term effort. What is needed is not more technology in education, but better alignment between *pedagogical values and cognitive design*. Learning requires attention. And attention requires friction—not constant stimulation.

One powerful intervention lies in *building attentional resilience.* Like physical stamina, attention can be trained. Practices such as deep reading, deliberate practice, reflective journaling, and mindfulness all strengthen the brain's capacity for sustained focus. Even simple acts—such as leaving the phone in another room while working—can create meaningful gains. But these practices require a cultural reframing. We must stop treating boredom as a failure and instead recognise it as an opportunity for mental deceleration. *Boredom is not the enemy of thought. It is its threshold.*

There is also a broader ethical imperative. If attention is a finite resource, then shaping how it is spent is a form of power. The current economy treats attention as a commodity—something to be harvested, sold, and optimised. But this commodification obscures the human cost. Every moment of distracted scrolling, every missed opportunity for reflection, is a subtraction from what could have been a moment of growth or insight. Reclaiming attention is not merely a lifestyle choice—it is an act of cognitive sovereignty.

Ultimately, the link between screen time, attention, and thought is not linear—it is ecological. These elements interact, reinforce, and reshape each other. Shorter attention spans do not just make us less patient; they make us less curious, less capable of grappling with complexity, less willing to pursue nuance. And that impoverishes not only our individual minds but our collective discourse.

The solution is not to romanticise a pre-digital past, but to demand a more intentional digital present. One in which attention is protected, not exploited. In which depth is valued, not penalised. In which tools are designed not just for engagement, but for *enrichment.* For in the end, the quality of our attention determines the quality of our thought. And the quality of our thought determines the quality of our lives.

## How Tech Shapes Thought Itself

When Marshall McLuhan famously declared that "the medium is the message," he pointed to something many still underestimate: *the way we absorb information is not neutral.* The form through which content reaches us subtly conditions how we engage with it—and ultimately, how we think. This insight, once confined to media theory seminars, is now urgent public knowledge. The proliferation of screens in daily life—from smartphones to tablets to laptops—has not merely changed what we access, but *how we read, how we remember, and how we reason.* We are not simply consuming information differently; we are *becoming different thinkers* as a result.

Reading on screens is cognitively distinct from reading on paper. Eye-tracking studies consistently show that people read digital text in an "F-pattern": scanning across the top line, then down the left margin, occasionally darting rightward but rarely moving through a page line by line. This skimming is not a quirk—it is a trained adaptation. Screen interfaces, filled with hyperlinks, buttons, alerts, and infinite scrolls, discourage deep linear reading. Instead, they train us to *scan for novelty*, to evaluate content by headlines and thumbnails, and to leap across fragments of information without integrating them. Over time, these behaviours calcify into *reading habits*, and those habits shape the cognitive structures that underlie comprehension and reflection.

The consequence is not just reduced retention—it is diminished *cognitive depth.* Deep reading—slow, immersive, analytical engagement with text—activates parts of the brain associated with inference, empathy, and conceptual integration. It builds mental models, encourages reflection, and fosters critical judgement. These processes are neurologically expensive; they require sustained attention and cognitive stamina. When reading is habitually shallow, the neural circuitry that supports deep reading weakens. As neuroscientist Maryanne Wolf puts it, the brain is plastic, and it will rewire itself to the modes of reading it practices most. If we teach it to skim, it becomes *a skimming brain.*

Memory, too, is reshaped by digital environments. With the promise of endless searchability, we now store less in our own minds and more in external systems. This is not inherently harmful—humans have always offloaded memory to tools, from oral traditions to written texts. But the nature of the offloading matters. The ubiquity of search engines like Google encourages *shallow encoding* of information: when we know we can look something up at any time, we are less likely to encode it meaningfully. This phenomenon, sometimes called the "Google Effect," shifts our cognitive energy away from internalisation and towards location tracking—knowing *where* to find knowledge rather than *what* it is or *how* it connects.

The implication is that memory becomes more fragmented. Long-term memory is not just about recall—it is the substrate of thought. Concepts must reside in the mind to be manipulated, synthesised, or questioned. If ideas are not internalised, reasoning becomes reactive rather than reflective. The mind becomes a conduit for content rather than a crucible for ideas. Philosopher John Dewey once argued that knowledge must pass through the "refining fire" of the mind to become insight. The risk today is that knowledge bypasses the fire altogether, flitting across attention without ever catching flame.

Reasoning itself—our ability to draw conclusions, evaluate claims, and form coherent arguments—is also being altered by screen habits. Social media, with its stream of declarative opinions and bite-sized hot takes, encourages a form of *reactive cognition*. Thought becomes performative: less about inquiry, more about signalling, affirmation, and belonging. Platforms reward speed and certainty, not nuance or curiosity. In such an environment, the capacity for dialectical reasoning—holding conflicting ideas, suspending judgement, seeking deeper synthesis—atrophies. The screen does not prevent thought; it *biases* it, nudging it toward immediacy, simplicity, and tribalism.

Of course, not all screen use is equal. Writing a long essay on a laptop requires different cognitive faculties than scanning headlines on a news app. But the *dominant patterns* of digital interaction—swiping, tapping, scrolling, toggling—favour modes of thought that are short-term, shallow, and externally anchored. Even the visual interface itself—the layout of apps, the shape of buttons, the palette of alerts—conveys subtle cues about what matters, what is urgent, and what should be clicked next. These cues do not just *reflect* our attention; they actively *sculpt* it. The architecture of a platform is a form of pedagogy. And we are its students, whether we realise it or not.

Consider how the interface of Twitter (now X) shapes the way people debate. The character limit restricts expression, encouraging aphorisms over argument. Threads, while a partial workaround, fragment ideas into digestible bites. The like and retweet buttons incentivise agreement over engagement. The public metrics create pressure to conform, perform, and escalate. This is not merely about platform features—it is about *cognitive conditions*. People are less likely to explore ideas they cannot articulate in a soundbite, or that risk social sanction. In such an ecosystem, reason becomes hostage to rhetoric.

Even attention spans themselves are recalibrated by screen-based consumption. The expectation of instant loading, push updates, and auto-play conditions the mind to anticipate novelty. Anything slow—reading a dense book, sitting with a difficult problem, enduring ambiguity—feels unusually effortful. What used to be normal cognitive friction is now experienced as intolerable lag. This change is especially visible in younger generations raised on screens. Teachers report a marked decline in students' ability to concentrate on extended tasks or follow multi-step arguments. The issue is not intelligence—it is *cognitive pacing*. The tempo of screen interaction rewires the internal rhythm of thought.

Yet the danger here is not technological, but unconscious. We tend to treat screens as content-delivery mechanisms, when in fact they are *cognitive environments*. They structure time, shape habits, mediate relationships, and condition perception. Just as the design of a classroom influences how students learn, or the layout of a city affects how people move, the architecture of our digital tools affects how we think. If these architectures remain invisible, they become *assumptions*. And unexamined assumptions are the most powerful of all.

There is, however, a path forward—not in rejection, but in *reflexivity*. Knowing how technology influences thought allows us to intervene. We can choose tools that encourage depth over noise. We can design interfaces that support reflection, not reaction. We can cultivate habits—like slow reading, handwritten notes, and screen-free periods—that re-anchor thought in embodied experience. Just as physical fitness requires deliberate training, cognitive depth requires intentional environments. *Screens do not have to shallow our minds; but if we ignore their influence, they will.*

In the end, the question is not whether technology affects thought. It always has. The printing press changed theology. The telegraph transformed diplomacy. The internet rewrote commerce. What matters is the *quality* of thought being fostered. Are we becoming more rigorous, more insightful, more connected to the ideas we engage with? Or are we becoming more fragmented, reactive, and superficial? The tools we use to think shape the kinds of thinkers we become. And that, in turn, shapes the kind of society we create.

If we are to defend the possibility of deep thinking—of real learning, real judgment, real insight—we must start by reclaiming awareness of the invisible environments shaping our minds. Not to reject screens, but to engage with them more consciously. Not to fear the digital, but to *design for cognition.* Only then can we ensure that the tools in our hands serve not just our attention, but our *intelligence.*

# Chapter 5
# Reclaiming Agency

The central peril of the digital era is not merely surveillance, distraction, or even addiction. It is passivity—not in the obvious sense of disengagement, but a more insidious surrender of choice to pre-configured defaults. Few of us consciously decide to unlock our phones dozens of times a day or to drift from a single message into a cascade of videos, losing track of our original intent. These behaviours are not the product of deliberate thought; they are engineered responses. With repetition, these unconscious patterns erect a framework for a life that feels increasingly automated, reactive, and disconnected from personal values.

Agency, in this context, is no abstract notion; it is tangible, measurable, and malleable. It can be diminished, reclaimed, or deliberately designed into one's daily routines. The urgency lies in the fact that most digital interactions are not neutral—they are carefully constructed choice architectures. Scroll lengths, colour schemes, button placement, notification timing—all of it nudges behaviour toward outcomes beneficial to the platform, not the user. Much like the proverbial frog in slowly warming water, we seldom notice the gradual constriction of our freedom. What starts as convenience subtly hardens into constraint.

Consider the average smartphone user, who spends nearly three hours daily on their device. These hours are not contiguous blocks of purposeful work; they are a mosaic of micro-engagements—moments stolen in queues, traffic lights, and in-between tasks. Such fragmentation erodes more than time; it erodes agency over attention. The pressing question is no longer whether technology consumes our focus, but whether it does so by deliberate design. Increasingly, it does.

Default settings exemplify this quietly coercive architecture: notifications activated, location services live, auto-play switched on. Each of these represents a pre-made choice—not by the user, but by designers. Few bother to change them, not from laziness but because our brains rely on cognitive heuristics: status quo feels safe, efficient, and implicitly recommended. Behavioural economists call this the "status quo bias," a powerful force shaping our routines without explicit consent. Left unchecked, it produces silent drift: a life guided as much by interface defaults as by conscious decision.

Reclaiming agency is therefore not a matter of "spending less time online," a blunt and moralistic framing that rarely works. A more effective question is: how can I design my digital environment to reflect my values rather than override them? This shifts the role of the user from passive consumer to active architect. Architecture, after all, is not about resisting the city; it is about shaping it thoughtfully. Similarly, digital design is not a moral battlefield but a terrain for intentional construction.

This perspective illuminates a crucial distinction between freedom from and freedom to. Many seek freedom from distraction, compulsive checking, or algorithmic nudges. But freedom to—freedom to focus, to rest, to read, to reflect—is more consequential. Agency is not merely the absence of interference; it is the presence of structures that enable intentional action. Here, boundaries are not arbitrary restrictions but deliberate scaffolds that support internal priorities. A tech-free bedroom is not punishment; it is a signal. A scheduled social-media window is not a limitation; it is a rhythm. These constraints stabilise attention and allow choice to flourish.

Digital boundaries, however, require supportive design. Relying solely on willpower is a losing strategy—frictionless interfaces almost always prevail. The more effective approach is to reintroduce friction deliberately: make unhelpful behaviours slightly harder, helpful ones slightly easier. Known as "digital friction," these tactics employ the same behavioural principles used to increase engagement, now repurposed to moderate it. Logging out after each session, removing app icons from home screens, or imposing time-limited access all introduce just enough resistance to disrupt automaticity. The goal is not elimination but a pause long enough to allow conscious choice.

Understanding design is equally crucial. Recognising how slot-machine psychology underpins infinite scroll, how red-badge notifications exploit FOMO, how social feedback loops reward performativity—these insights transform perception. Awareness diminishes compulsion. Cognitive liberation begins when users see the scaffolding beneath the interface. Education in this sense is neither moralising nor abstract; it is empowerment. Knowledge of the system yields leverage over it.

This is particularly vital in professional and academic settings, where the cost of distraction is not only wasted time but diminished cognitive output. Knowledge workers average less than three minutes on a single task before switching; students struggle to read more than a few pages without interruption. Such habits are structurally incompatible with deep work, original thought, or sustained analysis. Preserving intellectual labour demands intervention at the level of environmental design.

Agency also requires social infrastructure. One cannot reclaim attention entirely in isolation. Norms, peer expectations, and professional pressures reinforce default drift. Yet these norms can be redesigned: teams can establish communication windows, classrooms can implement device-free periods, families can create phone-free rituals. These are not nostalgic retreats; they are strategic reallocations of attention, optimised not for less technology but for more of what matters.

Finally, agency is proactive, not merely reactive. Waiting for a breakdown—anxiety, fatigue, or frayed relationships—places control downstream. True agency anticipates: "What do I want to enable?" Designing one's digital environment is a creative act, shaping both habit and identity. How we engage with technology is inseparable from how we engage with ourselves.

This chapter does not condemn technology nor prescribe simplistic detoxes. Its purpose is to illuminate the mechanics of digital systems and show how they can be structured in service of intentional living. From habit loops to strategic friction, from default settings to meaningful boundaries, agency is not mystical—it is architectural. And architecture, like life, begins with a question of purpose: what kind of existence should this structure support? Once that is clear, the tools to build it are already at hand.

## From Passive Use to Active Choice

Most people don't *choose* to spend over seven hours a day staring at screens. They drift into it. The drift is subtle, cumulative, and often unnoticed. It begins with a check of the time, followed by a glance at a notification, a quick response to a message, and before long, a thumb is scrolling, attention splintered, and an hour has vanished. This isn't willful indulgence—it's the product of *passive interaction with persuasive systems*. And because the behaviour doesn't feel "chosen," it also doesn't feel subject to revision. That illusion—that screen time is somehow happening *to us*—is perhaps the most dangerous of all. If we are to reclaim agency, the first task is to recognise that the problem is not just excessive usage, but *unconscious usage.*

Passive tech use is not characterised by duration but by *intentionlessness.* It occurs when we engage with our devices without a clear purpose, and continue engaging well beyond the original reason. This kind of use is often accompanied by emotional automation: reaching for the phone when anxious, bored, or momentarily still. In such moments, the device becomes a pacifier—an automatic response to discomfort or uncertainty. What begins as a coping mechanism quickly solidifies into a behavioural default. And the more frequently a habit is repeated in similar contexts, the more neurologically entrenched it becomes. *Passive use is not lazy; it is learned.*

What makes this so insidious is the way technology platforms are structured to reward it. Every frictionless swipe, infinite feed, and algorithmically-tuned "For You" page is designed to reduce the need for conscious initiation. In behavioural design, this is known as *reduction of activation energy*—the process of making a behaviour easier to perform, thereby increasing its frequency. This is useful when applied to beneficial habits (like brushing teeth or exercising), but dangerous when applied to content consumption. Passive use is encouraged not because it's good for the user, but because it *maximises dwell time*—a metric tightly correlated with ad revenue and platform growth.

Recognising unconscious habits requires a level of meta-awareness that few users are trained to cultivate. Most technology use is embedded within environments of distraction and speed. We use our devices while walking, waiting, commuting, eating, working, and even before sleeping. Rarely do we pause long enough to ask *why* we're reaching for the phone—or whether the usage aligns with our intentions. And herein lies the first pivot: from reactivity to reflection. The aim is not to become hyper-vigilant or self-critical, but to *restore visibility to behaviour that has gone opaque.*

One of the most effective ways to interrupt passive patterns is by introducing intentional prompts at the point of contact. This can be as simple as renaming a folder ("Why now?" instead of "Social"), moving apps off the home screen, or installing a lock screen reminder that asks, "What are you here for?" These subtle interventions serve as cognitive checkpoints—*a momentary invitation to reflect before indulging.* While small, they create the necessary pause in which choice can re-enter. Without such friction, the default wins.

More profoundly, intentional use requires the cultivation of *internal signals* to guide external engagement. In a passive loop, behaviour is triggered by external cues: a buzz, a badge, a ping. In an intentional loop, engagement is preceded by *internal alignment*—a decision made in light of what the user values or needs. This demands clarity not only about one's priorities, but also about *how technology supports—or sabotages—them.* A student who uses YouTube for tutorials but spirals into entertainment must differentiate between those modes of use. An executive checking email before bed must examine whether this enhances productivity or corrodes rest. These are not moral questions; they are architectural ones: *does the structure of your engagement serve your goals, or undermine them?*

It's also critical to acknowledge that passive use is not a purely individual failing. It is a *socially sanctioned default.* Entire workplace cultures reward availability over focus, encouraging employees to respond within minutes, regardless of task importance. Social norms reinforce always-on connectivity—answering late-night messages, documenting personal life for public platforms, and interpreting "seen" ticks as obligations to respond. To shift toward intentional use often requires not only personal discipline, but *cultural courage.* Choosing not to be immediately available, or not to engage with performative sharing, can feel like swimming against the current. But culture is not monolithic—it is made and remade by the behaviours we normalise.

Shifting to active choice doesn't mean abandoning technology; it means using it *on purpose.* This shift is anchored in two capacities: *discernment* and *design.* Discernment is the ability to distinguish between meaningful and mindless engagement, to notice when a swipe has become a spiral. Design is the ability to create systems—both internal and external—that support the former and disrupt the latter. This might mean scheduling app usage during defined windows, setting clear exit conditions for digital tasks, or deliberately designing moments of digital silence into one's day. These are not constraints; they are *enablers of conscious agency.*

Yet even intentional usage is vulnerable to backsliding if it relies solely on willpower. What's needed is a shift in *identity narrative.* Instead of merely setting behavioural goals ("I want to use my phone less"), users must adopt *identity-aligned frames* ("I am someone who protects my attention"). This shift reorients behaviour not around restriction but around self-concept. A person who sees themselves as a deep thinker, a present parent, or a focused creator will naturally evaluate digital choices through that lens. *When usage aligns with identity, the motivation is intrinsic, and the behaviour more durable.*

Intentional use also opens the door to *creative repurposing.* Just as we once adapted technologies like the printing press, the telephone, or radio to serve collective needs, we can reshape digital tools to foster reflection, learning, and meaningful connection. Note-taking apps can become repositories of insight, not just lists. Group chats can be repurposed as focused study or accountability spaces. Screen time reports can be interpreted not as guilt-inducing metrics but as *diagnostics for design refinement.* The key is not to reject digital life but to reclaim its architecture in service of *what we actually want from it.*

Ultimately, the shift from passive use to active choice is not a one-time epiphany but an ongoing discipline. It requires noticing the loops we didn't mean to enter, renegotiating our relationship with alerts, and continually asking: *Is this how I want to spend my attention?* Over time, this question becomes less effortful. Like any muscle, attention strengthens with use. And when reclaimed, it becomes more than a defence against distraction—it becomes the *engine of an intentional life.*

No app update or productivity hack will grant this kind of agency. It begins when we stop being passengers in our digital routines and start becoming *designers of our own attention.* The first step is awareness. The second is willingness. The rest is structure. And once the structure is in place, the user is no longer a subject of the system, but the author of their own engagement.

## Designing for Control

For many users, digital environments are not chosen; they are inherited. They open their phones, launch their browsers, scroll through feeds, and respond to alerts in spaces they never deliberately constructed. The home screen is populated with default apps, the email inbox is prioritised by opaque algorithms, and the platforms they frequent are designed less for productivity than for persistence of engagement. In this context, attention is not *spent*, it is *extracted.* And yet, the majority of users operate within these architectures without question, assuming that what is default is also neutral. It isn't. Defaults are decisions, and they are rarely made in the user's best interest. To reclaim intentionality in a digital world, one must begin not with discipline, but with *design.*

Designing for control means recognising that digital environments—like physical ones—shape behaviour. Just as a cluttered desk invites distraction and a well-lit kitchen invites cooking, so too does a notification-ridden home screen invite reactivity. The science of behavioural design, particularly as articulated by researchers like B.J. Fogg and Nir Eyal (ironically both contributors to persuasive tech), teaches us that environment often trumps motivation. People don't check their phones because they've planned to; they do so because the structure of the interface invites them to. *Small frictionless cues, repeated often enough, become default actions.* Thus, regaining control is not simply about reducing usage; it's about redesigning the paths that lead to unconscious engagement.

A foundational principle in this redesign is *stimulus control.* In psychological terms, stimulus control involves shaping the environment to cue desired behaviours while reducing the presence of cues that trigger unwanted ones. On a practical level, this could mean removing social media apps from the home screen, disabling auto-login features, or placing devices physically out of reach during focused work. These are not acts of deprivation, but of strategic alignment. When the design of an environment supports one's priorities, behaviour becomes more reflective, less reactive. This is *digital feng shui*—crafting digital spaces that support, rather than sabotage, the kind of person one intends to be.

Critically, this kind of control cannot be outsourced to platforms. The incentives of most major digital services are structured around engagement maximisation, not user empowerment. Their design choices—such as infinite scroll, autoplay, personalised feeds, and variable rewards—are optimised for time-on-platform, not wellbeing. Asking a platform to help users use it less is like asking a casino to optimise for moderation. Users must therefore act as their own architects, treating their devices not as finished products but as *editable environments.*

One of the most effective levers in this process is the creation of *deliberate friction.* This runs counter to the dominant design ethic of convenience, which posits that smoother is better, faster is smarter, and seamlessness is a virtue. But what we gain in speed, we often lose in intentionality. Introducing friction—through time limits, lockout periods, delayed access, or even requiring written reflection before launching certain apps—can serve as a crucial interruption to unconscious loops. For instance, a user might install an app blocker that asks them to type a 50-word justification before opening Instagram. This minor inconvenience is often enough to shift the brain from autopilot to awareness, triggering a reconsideration of the intended action. *The goal is not to eliminate use, but to restore agency to the moment of choice.*

Another design principle with transformative potential is *bundling.* This involves pairing digital engagement with a specific context or routine, rather than allowing it to seep into every moment. For example, designating 30 minutes each evening for recreational browsing on a laptop—rather than scattered throughout the day on a phone—can preserve both enjoyment and containment. Bundling reintroduces boundaries into what has become a boundaryless space. It mirrors how we treat other powerful stimuli: alcohol, sugar, entertainment. When these things are consciously timed and contextually placed, they serve pleasure; when they are always available, they dominate attention.

Crucially, digital control is not just about limiting input; it's also about curating output. Most users consume far more content than they actively seek. Algorithmic feeds, trending topics, autoplay chains—these are designed to lead users, not serve them. Taking back control requires shifting from a *pull-based model* (content seeking us) to a *push-based model* (we seek the content). This might mean unsubscribing from algorithmic timelines in favour of manual content selection, using RSS readers, or subscribing to high-quality newsletters instead of infinite feeds. It might mean choosing to *read longform over headlines*, or to *listen to full conversations over isolated clips*. When the user becomes the editor, not the consumer, the relationship to content transforms.

Of course, the most powerful digital environments are not visual—they are *temporal.* The structure of one's day is itself an interface. A person who begins the morning in reactive consumption (checking news, email, or social feeds) is effectively placing their cognitive architecture at the mercy of external input. The first 30 minutes of the day are a high-leverage period in shaping mood, focus, and intention. Designing for control means intentionally scripting this window—perhaps with reading, planning, or movement—before inviting the digital world in. The same principle applies to transitions between work blocks, meals, and sleep. Defaulting to screens in these moments is not neutral; it fragments attention and erodes rest. Thoughtful rituals—closing rituals for work, pre-sleep wind-downs, post-lunch tech breaks—create *breathing space* in a world that otherwise rushes to fill it.

Importantly, control does not mean isolation. Designing for mindful use can include digital tools that enhance self-awareness, such as screen time tracking apps, digital journals, and calendar-based time auditing. When used intentionally, these tools function as *mirrors*, not distractions. They surface patterns, prompt reflection, and help the user align their time with their values. The key distinction is whether the tool is *serving awareness or substituting for it.*

Some will argue that this level of customisation is impractical—that most people won't take the time to rewire their settings, app layouts, or routines. But this argument misunderstands the stakes. We do not make these changes for convenience. We make them because *attention is finite, and design is destiny*. If we do not design for focus, we default to distraction. If we do not build for clarity, we drift into confusion. The price of inaction is not just productivity—it is presence, depth, and the capacity to *know what we think before the world tells us what to think.*

There is also a broader cultural implication. As more individuals redesign their digital environments, they subtly shift norms. A team that normalises scheduled email responses rather than instant replies creates breathing room for deeper work. A family that places phones outside the dining room restores the table as a space of presence. These are not technological innovations; they are *design declarations.* They say: we decide what our tools are for. We shape the terms of engagement.

Designing for control is not about turning back the clock to a pre-digital world. It is about reclaiming authorship in a digital one. It is the difference between being an occupant and being an architect. Every setting we change, every default we override, every cue we remove or introduce—these are small but powerful acts of sovereignty. And while platforms will continue to optimise for more—more clicks, more views, more hours—the user who designs for enough will live differently. They will live by design, not by drift. And that, in the end, is the ultimate control.

## Digital Boundaries That Hold

Boundaries are not walls; they are decisions made visible. They are the lines we draw to signal what matters, to ourselves and to others. In the digital context, boundaries are often perceived as limitations—as things one must endure or deny oneself. But in reality, *well-designed boundaries are enablers.* They carve out space for presence, focus, and rest in an otherwise relentless stream of stimulation. The problem is not that we lack the capacity to be intentional with technology—it's that our environments often lack the architecture to support that intention. Most users do not consciously surrender their attention; they simply haven't placed anything in the way of its automatic extraction. The challenge, then, is to create *boundaries that hold*, not through sheer willpower, but through smart design and cultural clarity.

A digital boundary is effective only if it is *both respected and sustainable.* This requires moving beyond vague aspirations like "I'll use my phone less" to specific, rule-based structures that govern access and use. The brain thrives on predictability; boundaries that fluctuate or depend on mood collapse under pressure. Consider the difference between saying "no phone in the bedroom at night" and saying "I'll try not to scroll before bed." The former is behavioural architecture. The latter is a negotiation waiting to be lost. The psychology is clear: rules beat decisions. Especially when tired, stressed, or emotionally charged, the human brain struggles to choose wisely in the moment. *Pre-commitment replaces the burden of repeated judgement with the clarity of predetermined constraint.*

One of the most practical forms of digital boundary is the *tech-free zone.* This is a spatial rule, not a temporal one. It states: in this physical location, devices do not enter. Bedrooms, dining tables, meeting rooms, and bathrooms are common starting points. The power of this approach lies in its simplicity. Unlike timers or apps, spatial rules are visually reinforced. The absence of a phone on the table is both a signal and a safeguard. In families, such zones model presence for children; in workplaces, they re-establish shared attention as a norm. Over time, these zones create cognitive associations—spaces where the mind learns to expect depth, stillness, or connection, unmediated by screens.

Complementary to tech-free zones are *usage windows*—clearly defined periods in which engagement with digital devices is either permitted or discouraged. This tactic, borrowed from nutrition science (intermittent fasting), acknowledges that *when* we use matters as much as *how much.* Morning usage windows might be delayed to preserve clarity; evening windows might be closed to support sleep. Crucially, these boundaries must be aligned with natural energy rhythms and life responsibilities. A usage window that cuts across peak productivity hours or excludes necessary communication is unlikely to endure. The key is not maximal restriction, but *durable rhythm.* Many professionals find that even small temporal boundaries—no email before 9 a.m., no Slack after 6 p.m.—can radically transform their ability to focus and recover.

Some critics argue that such boundaries are artificial, that they impose an unnecessary rigidity on fluid modern life. But this misunderstands the function of boundaries. Their value lies precisely in their artificiality. Natural environments do not contain boundaries that protect our attention; if anything, they invite its constant dispersal. Without deliberate limits, *everything becomes available all the time*, and therefore *everything competes with everything.* The result is a form of cognitive erosion—always stimulated, rarely satisfied. Boundaries are the scaffolding that preserves cognitive sovereignty in an environment optimised for intrusion.

It's also important to recognise that *not all boundaries are created equal.* Some are externally imposed (parental controls, work policies), while others are internally chosen (self-imposed screen limits). The most effective boundaries tend to be those that align internal values with external signals. A person who values sleep, for instance, might place their phone in another room after 10 p.m., combining an internal motive with an environmental cue. In contrast, rules that are imposed without ownership—such as digital detox mandates or productivity challenges—often collapse under resentment or inconvenience. *Agency is not optional; it is the binding agent that holds the boundary in place.*

Technological tools can reinforce these decisions, but they must be chosen with care. Many so-called productivity apps are simply attention traps in disguise. A truly supportive tool *disappears when not needed*, and reappears only to reinforce intention. Examples include screen-dimming apps that reduce visual stimuli after certain hours, lockout timers that prevent access during deep work, and focus apps that visualise time spent on intentional versus unintentional use. These tools are not solutions in themselves; they are *scaffolds*, enabling users to practice and eventually internalise healthier patterns. As boundaries mature, users often report needing less external reinforcement—*the mind begins to protect what it values.*

In institutional and social contexts, boundary-setting requires cultural reinforcement. Consider the workplace that celebrates instant replies versus one that champions asynchronous communication. In the former, responsiveness becomes a performance metric; in the latter, it is seen as a threat to deep work. If digital boundaries are to hold, they must be *normalised*, not just permitted. Leaders who model boundaries—by turning off notifications during meetings, by not sending emails late at night, by defending focus time—set a tone that others follow. Culture, after all, is behaviour at scale. And *boundary-respecting cultures do not emerge by default; they are architected through example and expectation.*

Families, too, must negotiate these lines. The notion of a tech-free dinner is now a cultural cliché, but its execution remains rare. This is not due to lack of awareness, but to *lack of reinforcement.* A rule that is occasionally broken becomes harder to enforce than one never made. Consistency is the hidden currency of effective boundaries. Children learn not just what the rule is, but how serious the household is about maintaining it. Moreover, boundaries should evolve with age and context—not all family members have the same digital needs or capacities. What matters is not uniformity, but *clarity.* Boundaries that are clear, explained, and co-created are far more likely to endure than those that feel arbitrary or authoritarian.

There is also a deeper philosophical dimension at play. Digital boundaries are not merely about optimising focus or improving sleep. They are *ethical commitments*—acts of refusal in a culture of extraction. To set a boundary is to say: my attention is not for sale; my relationships deserve space; my thoughts require silence. These are not just productivity hacks; they are statements of personhood. In a society increasingly defined by availability, *choosing when not to be available is a radical act of self-definition.*

Still, boundaries are not magic. They do not eliminate temptation. They will be tested, stretched, sometimes ignored. The measure of their strength is not their perfection, but their resilience. A boundary that bends but reasserts itself is stronger than one that shatters at the first failure. This is why it's critical to build feedback loops into boundary-setting. Weekly reviews of screen time, intentional tech sabbaths, or self-reflection exercises can help users re-anchor their choices. Over time, *boundaries become habits, and habits become identities.* A person who once struggled to turn off their phone after work may come to see themselves as someone who *does not begin their evening with a screen.* This shift—from discipline to identity—is the final form of a boundary that holds.

As digital environments become ever more persuasive, passive boundaries will cease to suffice. The age of "use it wisely" is over. What's needed now is *architected intention*—clear, visible, defended limits that signal what we value, protect what we need, and reinforce who we are. Not boundaries imposed out of fear, but boundaries built with care. Not abstinence for its own sake, but space to think, relate, and rest. These are not indulgences. They are preconditions for a humane digital life. And they begin not with sweeping reforms, but with the smallest of acts: a phone left outside the room, a quiet hour reclaimed, a screen that stays dark long enough for thought to re-emerge. This is how boundaries begin. This is how they hold.

## The Power of Default Settings

Most people think of their digital preferences as something they actively choose. Yet, in the vast majority of cases, they don't. Whether it's the brightness of a screen, the frequency of notifications, the autoplay on a video platform, or the apps that appear on a phone's home screen, what shapes behaviour most consistently is not deliberate choice—it is *inherited design.* Defaults are powerful precisely because they operate below the threshold of scrutiny. What is pre-selected becomes what is used. What is presented first is what is accepted. In environments saturated by choice, *defaults are the invisible architecture of decision-making.*

Behavioural economists have long recognised this. Richard Thaler and Cass Sunstein, in their seminal work on "nudge theory," demonstrated how defaults—such as automatic organ donation opt-ins or pre-selected retirement contributions—dramatically influence outcomes without coercion. The same logic applies in the digital realm, but with even fewer checks. Most users do not review, let alone alter, the default settings of the platforms they use. Instead, they adapt themselves to the structure they are given. And while this may appear benign, it is often a subtle form of control. The problem is not that defaults exist, but that they *are rarely neutral.*

Consider the autoplay feature on video platforms. Its default setting—on—is not an innocent convenience. It is a deliberate design choice optimised to maximise time spent watching. A user who might otherwise pause to reflect or disengage is gently nudged into continuous consumption. Multiply this by billions of sessions per day, and the cumulative effect is enormous. People don't binge because they lack discipline; they binge because the architecture is primed for it. *The path of least resistance is rarely the path of most intention.*

Or take the case of app notifications. When a user installs a new app, the default behaviour is to request notification permissions immediately. Most users, eager to proceed, grant access reflexively. The result is an inbox of interruptions—alerts, badges, banners—many of which serve the platform more than the person. Few revisit these settings to refine or revoke access. What begins as convenience morphs into *habitual hijack*. The noise becomes normal. Silence feels strange.

This isn't mere oversight. It's strategy. In the digital economy, *attention is currency*, and platforms are designed to collect it as efficiently as possible. Defaults act as silent brokers in this exchange. They guide users toward behaviours that serve business models—longer sessions, more engagement, higher ad revenue. And because these choices are invisible, they rarely provoke resistance. A manipulative prompt feels invasive; a default feels like nothing at all. *That is its genius, and its danger.*

But if defaults can be used to extract value, they can also be reclaimed to *protect it.* One of the most empowering shifts a digital user can make is to treat every default setting as *a proposal, not a verdict.* The question is not "How do I work with this setup?" but "Why was this setup chosen, and for whose benefit?" This reframe invites scrutiny. And scrutiny is the precursor to agency.

Begin with the most basic: notification settings. Disable all non-essential alerts. Leave only the truly time-sensitive or human-critical ones—messages from loved ones, calendar reminders, task-specific alarms. Everything else is deferred or eliminated. Then move to home screen curation. Remove apps that trigger compulsive use from the first page. Make intentional use *easier* and reactive use *harder*. Resist the tyranny of immediacy by placing friction between impulse and access.

Next, review platform-level defaults. Turn off autoplay on streaming services. Set your phone to greyscale during focused work hours. Disable infinite scroll where possible. Mute algorithmic feeds in favour of chronological ones. Use browsers with privacy-first defaults. Opt out of data sharing when prompted. These are not drastic actions—they are *acts of return*. Returning to clarity, to calm, to choice. And crucially, to the knowledge that *you can override the preconfigured path*.

There's also a broader cognitive benefit at play. Reclaiming defaults requires noticing them. And noticing them trains attention to seek out the subtle forces shaping behaviour more generally. The user becomes a participant, not just a recipient. They begin to see how what appears natural is often designed; how ease and effort are engineered; how choices can be structured to guide, nudge, or trap. *This is metacognition applied to interface design*. And it cultivates the mental posture of sovereignty.

Of course, not all defaults are malicious or manipulative. Some are genuinely helpful. The goal is not paranoid opposition to all pre-set options. The goal is *discernment*. Does this setting serve my values, my attention, my energy? If not, it must be changed. If yes, it may stay. But nothing remains simply because it was there when you arrived. Nothing remains simply because someone else decided it should be so.

Organisations, too, are starting to recognise the significance of digital defaults. Companies like Slack, Basecamp, and Notion now allow for custom default settings that favour deep work—such as disabling notifications by default, offering dark modes to reduce cognitive strain, or allowing users to pre-select when they can be contacted.

These are not just usability features; they are *cultural signals*. They say: time matters, focus matters, people matter more than pings. And when leaders embrace these signals—by using them, modelling them, reinforcing them—they create environments where digital dignity becomes the norm rather than the exception.

Educational settings offer another powerful frontier. Teachers who disable autoplay on classroom devices, who structure digital tools to support curiosity rather than compulsion, send a subtle but crucial message: *you are not just a user—you are a learner, and your attention deserves protection.* In such environments, students begin to distinguish between intentional use and engineered engagement. They begin to ask better questions of their tools—and of themselves.

Ultimately, the power of default settings is not just about interface design. It is about *choice architecture at large.* Every aspect of our lives is structured by defaults: whether we sit or stand, scroll or pause, respond immediately or reflect first. These defaults can be designed *by others*—or reclaimed *by us.* And in a culture that profits from the erosion of attention, reclaiming is a political, psychological, and philosophical act.

No one escapes the influence of defaults. But anyone can interrogate them. Anyone can decide that attention is too valuable to be left to convenience. That presence is too sacred to be surrendered by default. And that design should begin not with what is easy, but with what is right.

So let the guiding principle be this: *no default goes unexamined.* Not because every change will transform your life. But because the act of examination *is itself the transformation.* It is a return to authorship. A reassertion of boundaries. A quiet refusal to let unseen choices shape a visible life. That is the power of defaults. And it belongs, ultimately, to the one who questions them.

# Chapter 6
# Attention is Your Currency

If money governs transactions in the marketplace, attention governs transactions with reality itself. Where attention flows, energy and behaviour inevitably follow. To direct it is to assign value—whether consciously or unconsciously—to what matters. This is no mere flourish of language; it is both a neurological and cultural fact. The objects of our attention shape neural pathways, bias memory, and mould identity. Attention is not simply a lens through which we perceive—it is a sculptor of who we become. In an era of digital surplus, where options multiply and interruptions are engineered, what we choose to notice carries extraordinary weight.

Attention is both scarce and potent. We inhabit an economy that extracts it, technologies that compete for it, and a culture that often undervalues it. Acts of awareness that were once spontaneous are now contested commodities, sold in milliseconds to the highest bidder. Autonomous attention is fragile; preserving it demands deliberate intention. And here, intention is far from a vague disposition—it is a disciplined, practised skill.

At the core lies a simple, yet profound premise: what you pay attention to, you become. Not metaphorically, but literally. Neural networks adapt to repeated engagement. When attention is consumed by fragmented, trivial stimuli—notifications, scrolling feeds, ambient drama—the mind adapts in kind: restless, impatient, shallow. Conversely, attention directed toward reflection, conversation, or deliberate challenge fosters a mind that mirrors that focus. In essence, attention is identity in motion.

Yet we rarely treat it with such care. We spend it casually, reactively, compulsively—tapping, swiping, skimming. The consequences are real and increasingly measurable. Studies link habitual digital distraction to heightened anxiety, diminished working memory, reduced creativity, and lower thresholds for boredom. Users are not merely overwhelmed; they are diluted. This is not a question of willpower or moral deficiency—it is structural. The system is engineered to fragment attention, and the toll is not just temporal; it is clarity, coherence, and inner steadiness.

Scattered attention begets scattered selves. Thoughts fragment, moods fluctuate, intentions blur. Stimulation masquerades as significance, urgency as importance. Life is lived on partial alert—emotionally thin, perpetually interrupted. Wellness rhetoric often misattributes this state to stress or burnout, but the root cause is unregulated attention. We are not merely tired; we are pulled. Not merely anxious; we are attuned to too much.

Time management alone cannot remedy this. The true discipline is attentional economy: allocating cognitive currency where it counts. The modern challenge is not the abundance of input, but the scarcity of discrimination. Mindfulness transcends cliché to become survival skill—the capacity to notice what is happening as it unfolds, without surrendering to it.

Intentional attention, like a muscle, strengthens with exercise and atrophies through neglect. This chapter introduces practices not as isolated tricks but as enduring scaffolds for attentional hygiene. Pausing before task-switching, naming distractions, cultivating dedicated mono-tasking intervals—these are not novelties, but small, repeated investments whose cumulative effect outweighs hours of distracted effort.

Attentional budgeting mirrors financial management. Just as one would not spend indiscriminately in a shop, attention should not be squandered on every ping, feed, or notification. Unlike money, depletion is often invisible until signs of burnout, irritability, or aimlessness emerge. A budgeted approach involves prioritising attention for what aligns with values, goals, and cognitive rhythms: recognising what deserves full presence, what can proceed on autopilot, and what must be deliberately ignored.

Budgeting is not deprivation; it is agency. It permits focus, leisure, depth, and restorative rest. It separates noise from signal, enabling conscious engagement instead of passive absorption. This is not a repudiation of technology, but a recalibration: a refusal to surrender the frontlines of mental life to algorithms optimised for retention rather than reflection.

Attention is precious not because it is rare, but because it is formative. Where attention goes, life follows. Relationships flourish or wither, projects succeed or falter, ideas deepen or dissipate according to how attentional energy is allocated. It is the lever through which all experience is shaped, and thus it must be protected—not only from intrusion, but from gradual erosion.

This is not a call to minimalism for its own sake, nor an indictment of screens and software. It is a call to reclaim authorship of the attentional self, to notice how life is outsourced to inputs, to re-enter the loop of intention, observation, and choice. The direction of attention is the direction of life.

Everything in the following chapter is anchored in this premise. The aim is not only to recover focus, but to cultivate a framework for living as if attention matters—because it does. Not merely to accomplish more, but to become more aligned with what one values. In a world that constantly extracts attention, the most radical act may be to spend it wisely. This chapter offers a guide to doing precisely that.

## What You Pay Attention To, You Become

The human mind is not a passive container—it is a sculptor, continuously shaping itself according to where attention is directed. Neurologically, psychologically, and even morally, *what we consistently attend to rewires our perception of reality, our emotional dispositions, and ultimately our sense of self.* In a world saturated with digital stimuli, engineered to seize attention and hijack focus, this has profound implications. The consequences are not just momentary lapses in concentration, but a slow, cumulative shaping of who we are becoming.

The claim that attention shapes identity is not a rhetorical flourish; it is a neuroscientific fact. The brain's plasticity—the capacity to physically restructure itself in response to experience—is directed by attentional selection. When we repeatedly focus on certain types of information or behaviours, neural pathways associated with those experiences strengthen. Attention is the mechanism by which we lay down memory, form habits, and reinforce patterns of thought. In effect, attention *instructs the brain on what to prioritise and preserve.* Just as muscles grow with targeted exercise, mental faculties develop in accordance with what we consistently focus on.

This has always been true. But in previous eras, attention was governed more by intention than by automation. It was more likely to be directed by personal goals, real-time environments, and interpersonal obligations. Today, however, attention is routinely diverted by platforms, pings, banners, feeds, and alerts—each optimised for interruption, not intention. We have entered what could be described as a post-autonomous attentional age, in which focus is no longer assumed to be self-directed. Instead, it is a resource *captured by design.*

The implications of this shift are more than behavioural—they are ontological. If attention is what we use to navigate, interpret, and engage with the world, then losing control over it amounts to losing control over the construction of the self. This is not merely a concern for philosophers. It is an everyday crisis. Consider the average user who, on waking, reaches for their phone and begins scrolling through social media. This act, seemingly trivial, quickly becomes habitual. What begins as checking updates evolves into *daily cognitive framing*: setting emotional tone, social comparisons, ideological exposures, and worldview cues—before even stepping out of bed. What gets repeated embeds. And *what embeds becomes default.*

Digital platforms are not inherently harmful in this regard. But their incentive structures are not neutral. Engagement is the metric that drives design, and engagement is most reliably harvested through emotional arousal—outrage, desire, fear, envy. Over time, this shapes not only what we consume, but *what we expect.* The threshold for stimulation rises. The tolerance for slowness, ambiguity, or complexity diminishes. And because attention is a limited resource, what is fed to it displaces what is not. *Sustained reflection, slow reading, deep listening—these begin to feel effortful, even alien, not because we lack capacity, but because we have misallocated our attention budget.*

This is where the myth of "just being informed" breaks down. Passive consumption is not neutral. The endless drip of novelty, crisis, and commentary rewires not only what we know, but how we know. To be exposed repeatedly to performative content, tribal antagonism, or algorithmic manipulation is to slowly absorb the logic of those structures. We begin to mirror the environments we inhabit. Cynicism becomes reflexive. Attention spans erode. Our sense of agency diminishes. Not because we decided to become distracted, but because *distraction became the dominant mode of engagement.*

This erosion of attentional agency also affects values. What we pay attention to becomes emotionally charged. Repeated exposure lends familiarity, and familiarity breeds comfort—even when the content is toxic. If outrage-inducing content garners the most attention, it becomes perceived as the most important. If trivial entertainment is the most frequent input, it becomes the default context. Over time, *we confuse what is salient with what is significant.* And because attention validates content—through clicks, likes, views—it also subtly signals what matters. Identity, then, is not just formed by inner reflection, but *moulded by what receives repeated external focus.*

Importantly, this process is rarely conscious. We do not wake up and choose to dilute our capacity for focus, depth, or care. But through daily habits, left unexamined, we drift into identities built not by design, but by default. Philosopher Harry Frankfurt wrote of "bullshit" not as lies, but as discourse indifferent to truth. In the attentional economy, we risk becoming *indifferent to coherence.* When content is consumed for distraction rather than understanding, we form mental models based on fragments, not frameworks. The cost is not just cognitive—it is existential. *We lose the narrative thread of who we are and what we stand for.*

There is also a moral dimension. Attention is how we bestow dignity. To listen fully, to observe patiently, to witness without distraction—these are acts of presence that affirm both the subject and the self. When attention is split, withheld, or automated, relationships suffer. Not only with others, but with ourselves. We become strangers to our own impulses, anxieties, and aspirations—too busy to notice, too fragmented to integrate. To reclaim attention is not just to boost productivity. It is to *reclaim self-authorship.*

This raises a practical question: can we choose what we attend to, in a landscape built to override choice? The answer is yes—but with effort. Regaining attentional sovereignty requires awareness of how easily it is hijacked. It begins with naming the forces at play: the dopamine incentives of endless scroll, the manufactured urgency of push notifications, the false sense of productivity from shallow multitasking. Once these patterns are recognised, they can be interrupted. More importantly, they can be replaced.

Intentional redirection of attention is not merely about resistance. It is about cultivation. Choosing where to place attention becomes an act of *curation for the mind.* What ideas do we want to engage? What relationships do we want to nurture? What skills do we want to grow? None of these are compatible with perpetual distraction. They require not just time, but *undivided awareness.* And because awareness is fragile in digital environments, it must be protected through deliberate design—tech-free rituals, focused work sprints, ambient interruption blockers, and above all, a shift in internal narrative from reaction to intention.

Some may argue that the digital age is too far gone for such control to be reclaimed. But the neuroplasticity that allowed for erosion also allows for recovery. Attention, like a muscle, regains strength with targeted use. Even small acts of attentional discipline—reading a book without switching tabs, having a conversation without checking a phone, noticing a craving without acting on it—begin to rewire the self toward presence. These acts compound. They reclaim cognitive real estate. And eventually, they restore the individual as the agent of their own awareness.

In this sense, attention is both the mechanism and the reward. To pay attention is to honour reality. To focus deeply is to remember that thought can be rich, that moments can be meaningful, and that identity is not a brand, but a living narrative shaped by presence. What we attend to, we amplify. And what we amplify, we become.

The question, then, is not whether our attention is being spent. It is whether it is being spent *on purpose.* Because if attention is currency, then what we choose to pay for defines the wealth of our inner life. And if identity is formed by accumulation, then each click, each scroll, each moment of presence or absence, is a micro-investment in the self we are building. That investment is either conscious or automatic. But it is never neutral. The self is always under construction. And *attention is the blueprint.*

## Mental Clutter and Emotional Noise

The modern mind is not overburdened because it works too hard, but because it *processes too much.* Every day, we wake to a deluge of digital input—notifications, headlines, messages, updates, reminders—each demanding micro-attention, each fragmenting our internal stillness. What once passed for idle mental space has become a noisy corridor of half-finished thoughts, emotional residue, and competing demands. The consequence is not merely distraction. It is chronic mental clutter, with a cognitive and emotional cost few have fully reckoned with.

The average person now consumes the equivalent of 74 gigabytes of information per day—a figure that has more than quintupled since the 1980s. Yet the brain has not evolved at the same pace. The neural architecture responsible for attention, memory, and emotional regulation remains largely unchanged from our pre-digital ancestors. We are primates designed for depth, thrust into a world designed for volume. It is this mismatch—between what our minds are built for and what our devices deliver—that lies at the heart of modern psychological fatigue.

Cognitive overload is not a theoretical concept. It is observable in rising anxiety rates, diminishing working memory, and the inability to sustain focus on a single task without the ambient pull of background tabs. But what's less discussed is the *emotional noise* this constant stimulation generates. Every interruption—however brief—forces a reorientation of attention, draining finite mental energy. This phenomenon, known as "attention residue," lingers even after we switch tasks, leaving our thoughts cloudy and our emotions unsettled. When multiplied across dozens—or hundreds—of micro-interruptions per day, it creates a baseline of unease that is easily misattributed to external stressors. But in truth, *much of our modern anxiety is self-inflicted, ambient, and digitally mediated.*

Even so-called passive scrolling is not emotionally neutral. The brain does not distinguish between real and virtual stimuli when it comes to arousal. A provocative post, a tragic news story, an envy-inducing highlight reel—all trigger genuine affective responses. These moments layer atop each other, accumulating without integration, resolution, or reflection. The result is an *unprocessed emotional backlog,* which lingers beneath conscious awareness, manifesting as restlessness, irritability, or a vague but persistent sense of overwhelm.

Consider the design of most social and content platforms. They are not structured around cognitive clarity, but around *engagement loops.* Infinite scroll, autoplay, algorithmic personalisation—these are not benign tools; they are engineered frictionlessly to capture attention and prolong use. But prolonged use does not equate to meaningful use. Instead, it often results in *information snacking*: a consumption pattern where the mind skips from one low-nutrient item to the next without digestion. Just as diets high in sugar and saturated fat produce metabolic disorder, mental diets high in novelty and stimulation produce *psychological inflammation*—a state of cognitive bloating, mental fatigue, and mood instability.

What makes this dynamic more insidious is its normalisation. We have come to mistake busyness for relevance, connectivity for closeness, and stimulation for satisfaction. There is little room in this schema for mental stillness, let alone the deliberate cultivation of it. Yet *mental stillness is not a luxury—it is a prerequisite for emotional coherence and psychological resilience.* Without it, the mind becomes a crowded house with no silent room, a place where every window is open, letting in wind, noise, and debris.

Emotional noise, then, is not simply about volume—it's about *lack of resolution.* When stimuli accumulate faster than they can be metabolised, the emotional system is placed under continuous load. It never has the opportunity to process, release, and return to baseline. This is particularly relevant to digital environments where the ratio of input to reflection is so skewed. A single hour on a content-rich platform might expose a user to hundreds of emotional cues—joy, outrage, sadness, desire, confusion—without context, continuity, or closure. Over time, this creates what some psychologists refer to as *emotional compression*: an experience of feeling everything and nothing simultaneously. The system is so overstimulated it loses its discriminative power.

This compression is a contributing factor to modern burnout. Not just the workplace variety, but *existential burnout*—the condition of being alive in a world that constantly solicits your attention but rarely offers meaning. When every moment is mediated, and every platform optimised for distraction, it becomes harder to locate the signal in the noise, to separate what matters from what is merely salient. This leads to a form of low-grade despair—not loud enough to be named, but deep enough to erode one's sense of vitality and direction.

Part of the solution lies in *intentional subtraction*. Just as clarity in writing often comes from removing unnecessary words, clarity in thought often comes from reducing unnecessary input. This does not mean rejecting technology altogether. Rather, it means *designing interaction boundaries that respect the limits of the human mind.* It means creating rituals of cognitive hygiene: setting periods of non-consumption, instituting boundaries around device use, and cultivating habits that promote depth over novelty. For instance, reading a physical book without background tabs open is no longer just a literary preference—it is a cognitive intervention. Likewise, taking a walk without headphones or resisting the reflex to check news feeds in idle moments is not just a lifestyle tweak—it is *a reclaiming of psychological sovereignty*.

These practices may seem small, but they compound. They create the mental whitespace necessary for clarity to emerge. And clarity is the antidote to emotional noise. When we create conditions for the mind to settle, the unresolved fragments of our inner experience begin to cohere. We start to notice what we've been feeling. We recover our sense of inner signal. And from there, we can respond to the world with discernment rather than reactivity.

The stakes are not just personal. Societies are shaped by what their members are capable of attending to. A culture unable to think clearly or feel deeply is vulnerable to manipulation, distraction, and demagoguery. The maintenance of democracy, civility, and collective meaning requires *citizens who can hear themselves think*. And this begins with managing the internal environment—reducing the mental clutter, quieting the emotional static, and restoring the conditions for coherent thought.

To do this well requires something rare today: *deliberate attentional curation*. Not everything deserves our eyes. Not every ping warrants our response. The most urgent thing is often not the most important thing. By learning to separate the two—through practice, design, and self-respect—we re-establish the mental clarity needed not just for focus, but for flourishing.

In the end, peace of mind is not a function of what we escape, but of what we allow in. And in a world that profits from our overstimulation, reclaiming clarity is not just an act of wellness. *It is an act of quiet rebellion.*

## Intentional Attention as a Practice

One of the most overlooked facts of the digital age is also one of the most transformative: *attention is trainable*. While most people treat their attention as an involuntary reflex—hijacked by whatever is loudest, newest, or nearest—the reality is that it can be shaped like any other faculty. But unlike reflexes, which are hardwired and automatic, *intentional attention is cultivated*. It requires effort, design, and, most critically, *practice*. In a world built to exploit distraction, this practice becomes not just therapeutic but essential—both for personal agency and cognitive sovereignty.

At the heart of mindfulness is a deceptively simple act: to notice. But in a saturated environment, noticing is no longer passive—it is radical. To direct your gaze consciously, to remain with a thought, a sensation, or a decision without fleeing into tabs or tasks, is to swim against a strong current. Most people have never been taught to stay. They're trained, often unconsciously, to flit. This is not merely a matter of habit. It's a matter of neural programming. The more frequently attention is diverted, the more those neural pathways are reinforced. The mind becomes what it practises, and what most modern minds practise is *fragmentation.*

Mindfulness training—whether through formal meditation, contemplative walking, or deliberate sensory awareness—serves as a counterweight to this drift. It interrupts the reflexive pull of reactivity and replaces it with *presence.* Not the vague, romanticised version often peddled by pop psychology, but the gritty, moment-to-moment discipline of *returning.* Again and again, to this breath, this word, this task. There is no glamour to it. No fireworks. Just the slow, deliberate restoration of attentional integrity.

The science here is robust. A growing body of neuroimaging studies reveals that consistent mindfulness practice strengthens the prefrontal cortex—the brain region associated with executive function, emotional regulation, and sustained focus—while reducing the activity of the default mode network, which governs mind-wandering and rumination. In other words, *mindfulness rewires the brain away from distraction and toward directed consciousness.* Not permanently, but cumulatively. Like a muscle, attention grows in precision and endurance the more it is used with intent.

But mindfulness is not just about individual moments of focus. It is also about *meta-awareness*—the capacity to notice when you are no longer paying attention, and to reorient without judgement. This is the skill that makes attention dynamic rather than brittle. Anyone can concentrate for a moment. What matters is the ability to detect when that concentration has slipped and to recover it without spiralling into self-criticism or avoidance. This alone is a quiet revolution in a culture conditioned to equate attention with perfection.

To bring this into everyday life, consider the act of checking your phone. Mindfulness does not require that you stop this behaviour, but that you *notice it as it begins.* The moment your hand moves toward your device—what triggered it? Boredom? Uncertainty? Emotional discomfort? The aim is not to moralise your actions, but to illuminate them. Most digital behaviours thrive in the dark. They survive because they remain unseen by the very person enacting them. Once noticed, they lose their grip. This is not willpower. It is *witnessing.*

Some of the most effective mindfulness practices do not look like meditation at all. They look like *design choices.* Placing your phone in another room while working. Using analogue tools for tasks that don't require the internet. Creating rituals of beginning and ending your day with non-digital activities—writing by hand, stretching, walking, reading physical books. These are not aesthetic preferences. They are cognitive scaffolding. They give the brain room to stabilise before it is pulled into digital flow states. And they preserve attention not just as a resource, but as a *moral force*—a way of directing energy toward what you value.

This reveals a deeper truth: *intentional attention is an ethical act.* Where you place your awareness is a declaration of what you consider meaningful. To give your attention mindlessly—to noise, to provocation, to distraction—is to allow external forces to shape your interior world. But to give it mindfully—to ideas, to people, to presence—is to affirm a sense of internal authorship. You begin to reclaim not just what you do, but who you are becoming.

Of course, the discipline of attention does not flourish in isolation. It needs *environmental support.* It is easier to remain present when your tools are aligned with your intentions. A phone with grayscale display. A browser stripped of algorithmic recommendations. A desktop without distracting icons. These are not gimmicks. They are *architectures of attention.* Just as urban design influences physical behaviour—where people walk, linger, gather—digital design influences mental behaviour. And the more deliberately we shape those environments, the more resilient our attention becomes.

Still, mindfulness is more than a collection of hacks. It is a practice of relating to experience with clarity and care. At its best, it helps surface the subterranean patterns that drive unconscious choices. That flicker of irritation when delayed. That impulse to self-soothe with screen time. That refusal to be bored. With practice, these impulses are no longer automatic. They are observed. And once observed, they become optional.

This is not about becoming perfect or serene. It is about becoming *less divided.* Fragmented attention leads to fragmented selfhood. But mindful attention restores the sense of continuity between intention and action. It closes the gap between knowing and doing. The moments become more real, not because they are more dramatic, but because you are actually *there* for them.

There is a kind of quiet power in this. A person who trains their attention does not need to chase motivation. They rely instead on orientation. Their compass is internal, not algorithmic. They choose what to amplify and what to mute. And in doing so, they begin to rewrite their experience of time itself—not as a stream of interruptions, but as a field of presence.

In a digital culture that monetises distraction, reclaiming attention is a radical act. But it is also a deeply human one. To be mindful is not to withdraw from life, but to *step into it with your eyes open.* To notice the texture of things. The rhythm of thought. The breath between words. And through this noticing, to recover something that constant stimulation has obscured: *the ability to care*—not reactively, but deliberately.

Mindfulness, then, is not the goal. It is the gate. It leads to a form of attention that is anchored, volitional, and expansive. And it reminds us that while the external world may not stop demanding our awareness, *we can still choose where to place it.* With practice, that choice becomes more frequent. With time, it becomes more natural. And with enough care, it becomes the foundation of a life lived awake.

## The Attention Budget

It is no longer time that we lack. It is attention. In a world where digital tools have democratised productivity and information is available in excess, what differentiates the focused from the frazzled is not hours on the clock, but the ability to *allocate attention with intention.* Like any scarce resource, attention demands management. Yet unlike money, which most people have at least been taught to budget, attention is often spent impulsively, reactively, and without record. The result is not just distraction—it is depletion. And over time, it becomes identity erosion: the slow dilution of what we truly value, replaced by what persistently demands our gaze.

Psychologists have long likened attention to currency. You *pay* attention. You *spend* time. These metaphors are not incidental. They point to the transactional nature of perception in a stimulus-rich world. Every moment of focus is a trade-off. To attend to one thing is to ignore countless others. This is the structure of all prioritisation. But unlike money—which typically leaves a visible trail—attention leaves few receipts. Most of it disappears into the ether of background scrolling, ambient noise, and unexamined digital habits. And that invisibility is part of the problem: *you cannot manage what you do not measure.*

The average person now consumes more than 34 gigabytes of information per day—enough to overload a laptop within a week. But few of us pause to consider how this volume affects not just our memory or comprehension, but the very way we *value experience.* An attention budget, then, is not merely a metaphor. It is a design imperative. It asks: *What are you giving your cognitive resources to? Does that align with who you want to become?*

The first step in budgeting attention is distinguishing between *intentional focus* and *attentional leakage.* Intentional focus is directed energy—it has a purpose, a target, and often a boundary. Attentional leakage, by contrast, is what happens in the margins: the five-minute check-ins that stretch into lost afternoons, the notifications that redirect your mental state without consent, the low-grade cognitive drag of being perpetually partially aware. Individually, these moments seem inconsequential. Cumulatively, they form the texture of your mental life.

Research from Stanford University has demonstrated that high media multitaskers—those who frequently divide their attention between multiple streams—perform worse on tests of working memory and sustained focus. More tellingly, they *believe* they are more productive, even as their actual cognitive performance declines. This gap between perception and performance reveals something deeper: *attention is not just about discipline. It is about awareness.* You cannot protect what you are unaware is being taken.

This is why the metaphor of budgeting matters. When people sit down to budget their finances, they must first examine where their money currently goes. The same is true of attention. Until you audit where your hours drift—what apps you default to, what content loops you fall into, what environments foster slippage—any attempt to reclaim attention will be theoretical at best. But once mapped, attention becomes something malleable. You can reallocate. You can design friction. You can, over time, replace reflexes with rituals.

A well-structured attention budget, like a financial one, includes both *non-negotiables* and *discretionary spending*. Non-negotiables might include deep work, focused reading, restorative rest, meaningful conversation—these are the cognitive equivalents of fixed expenses. They ground your attention in what matters. Discretionary attention might include light entertainment, social media, idle browsing—none of which are inherently harmful, but which require containment. The problem is not their existence. It is their excess.

Technology companies understand this perfectly. Many default interfaces are designed not to support budgeting, but to *obscure cost*. Infinite scrolls, autoplay videos, algorithmic feeds—they all function to sever awareness from expenditure. You do not see the tally rise. You do not feel the cumulative erosion. This is why reclaiming an attention budget also means *redesigning default environments*. App timers, website blockers, focus modes, notification muting—these are not crutches. They are boundary tools. They give your intentions teeth.

But there is a more subtle layer to attention budgeting that deserves emphasis: *not all forms of focus are equal in cognitive return*. Some tasks drain, while others restore. Some offer shallow stimulation, others generate deep satisfaction. A healthy attention budget accounts for *qualitative difference*, not just quantity. Ten minutes spent watching an anxiety-inducing news cycle is not the same as ten minutes spent walking in silence. Thirty minutes doomscrolling is not the same as thirty minutes creating something original. This is where insight must override instinct.

Many productivity systems encourage people to manage time in blocks. Yet few encourage them to manage *mental states*. You may schedule a task, but have you budgeted the attention *quality* required to complete it well? Focused writing, for instance, demands a clean attentional context—minimal intrusion, cognitive freshness, emotional stability. Responding to emails, by contrast, may tolerate more ambient noise. A true attention budget does not just allocate minutes. It allocates *minds*.

To operationalise this, consider creating *attention tiers*. Tier 1 includes cognitively demanding tasks requiring deep focus and limited disruption. Tier 2 includes moderate-focus activities that permit mild multitasking. Tier 3 includes low-impact activities that may be reactive or restorative. Once identified, these tiers allow you to match tasks with attention states more precisely. But they also help you identify mismatches—when you are attempting a Tier 1 task in a Tier 3 environment, for instance, and repeatedly failing not because you lack ability, but because your context is misaligned.

What distinguishes great thinkers, creators, and problem-solvers is not that they have more time, but that they *spend their attention with discernment*. They don't just prioritise tasks. They prioritise *mental readiness*. They learn to protect the hours in which they are most alert, most original, most emotionally attuned—and reserve them for what matters. In doing so, they preserve not just productivity, but *mental clarity*.

There is also an existential layer to the attention budget that transcends efficiency. To budget attention is to assert agency in an environment increasingly designed to undermine it. It is to say: *my mind is not up for auction*. In this way, budgeting attention is not a technical exercise. It is a philosophical stance. You decide what to give yourself to. You decide what will occupy your awareness. And over time, these decisions *define you*.

This is why mindfulness, introduced earlier, is such a critical companion to budgeting. Awareness precedes allocation. You cannot reorient attention without first noticing where it flows, and why. But once you do, budgeting becomes not restrictive but *liberating*. You begin to live days that feel *chosen* rather than consumed.

Ultimately, a well-calibrated attention budget is not about cutting distraction for its own sake. It is about creating a mental economy in which *depth, clarity, and care can thrive*. In that space, you not only become more effective. You become more *yourself*. Less fragmented, more anchored. Less reactive, more sovereign.

And that is the real promise of budgeting attention—not just better results, but a better relationship with reality. One in which the mind is not a passive surface absorbing whatever arrives, but a skilled steward choosing what to amplify and what to release. In an age of engineered distraction, that is a rare and radical competence—one well worth investing in.

# Chapter 7
# Mindful Tech Habits That Stick

The challenge has never been awareness. Most people already know they spend too much time online. They are not short of tips, techniques, or intentions. What they lack is follow-through—behavioural durability. The deeper problem is not failing to start new habits, but failing to sustain them. Yet this failure does not indicate weak will or laziness; it reflects a more profound misjudgement: the belief that meaningful change springs from occasional resolve rather than from repeated rhythm. Lasting behaviour is shaped less by bursts of effort than by thoughtful design.

This chapter opens with a simple, often overlooked truth: rituals outperform resolutions. A resolution is a spike of effort—motivated, idealistic, and usually unsustainable. A ritual, by contrast, is a repeatable scaffold, a form we give to time that slowly shapes us in return. Resolutions demand grand gestures; rituals demand consistency. One burns quickly, the other builds permanence. In the realm of digital wellbeing, this distinction is crucial. Deciding to "cut back" on screen time or "be more mindful" is insufficient. Without embedding behaviours into structured patterns, intentions evaporate. Rituals convert attention into architecture.

The psychology behind this is well established. Research on habit formation, notably the work of Wendy Wood and B.J. Fogg, demonstrates that behaviours repeated in consistent contexts become automatic. Intensity is unnecessary; structure suffices. Yet most digital habits emerge without intention or design. They are reactions to notifications, mood-driven coping mechanisms, or unconscious defaults. Many attempts to reform them fail because they seek to uproot reflexes without planting coherent alternatives. Habits cannot be erased; they can only be overwritten.

Precision is key. Effective behavioural change starts with one micro-adjustment at a time. Micro-habit stacking—linking small, specific behaviours to existing routines—offers greater longevity than sweeping lifestyle changes. For instance, placing your phone on a shelf before making morning coffee may seem trivial. Yet, repeated daily, it becomes a pre-commitment cue—a frictionless ritual that enforces boundary-setting without heroic resolve. Over time, such cues accumulate into environments that support, rather than undermine, intention.

Another principle is the power of keystone habits—small actions that create ripple effects across other behaviours. In digital hygiene, a keystone habit might be establishing a "last screen" rule before bed or relying on an analogue alarm clock to avoid morning phone temptation. These small shifts can transform sleep quality, mood, attention, and even self-perception. Scale is less important than centrality; keystone habits reshape context and redirect behaviour.

Even well-crafted rituals require feedback. Change is impossible without tracking. Contemporary self-tracking, however, is often surveillance-oriented: step counters, productivity dashboards, screen-time graphs that feel accusatory rather than empowering. The outcome is guilt without insight or metrics without meaning. This chapter advocates light-touch tracking—low-friction, reflective methods that illuminate patterns without becoming punitive. End-of-day check-ins, brief journaling on digital wins and slips, or qualitative self-observation foster behavioural awareness, not obsession.

Habits do not form in abstraction. They are shaped by cues, context, and cognitive load. If your environment is designed for distraction—phones always within reach, browsers open to temptation, days punctuated by pings—even the best intentions will falter. Sustainable tech habits require ecosystem redesign. It is not just what you do differently, but where and when you do it. Morning rituals, evening wind-downs, tech-free transitions: these practices reinforce identity more than time management. They remind you who you are choosing to be.

Philosophically, habits are enactments of identity. Every repetition votes for the person you are becoming. A daily ritual of digital restraint is not merely a productivity tactic; it is an act of self-definition. Attention management becomes agency. Small victories over reactivity, repeated consistently, recalibrate your sense of control. The internal narrative shifts from "I can't help it" to "I am someone who chooses." This is not motivational fluff—it is behavioural momentum.

Yet habit is fragile. Change requires friction, but not all friction is equal. The goal is not to eliminate discomfort but to reduce decision fatigue. Habits stick when anchored in cues, scaffolded by routines, and shielded from sabotage. A few well-chosen rituals, repeated until automatic, cease to compete for cognitive bandwidth. Behaviour becomes second nature—like brushing teeth.

It is also worth correcting a common misconception: sustainable habit change need not always feel joyous, nor does struggle signal failure. Research in behavioural economics, from Kahneman and Thaler, shows that defaults guide behaviour more reliably than stated preferences. People do what is easiest to repeat, not necessarily what they say they want. Designing tech habits that endure, therefore, requires ease, clarity, and minimal ambiguity. Vague or mood-dependent behaviours rarely survive long term.

This chapter argues not only for building better habits but for respecting the psychology of change. Friction where it matters, ease where it counts. Start small, but pursue coherence. Track progress without fixation. Build systems that reinforce your values.

Mindful tech habits that endure are not born of heroism; they arise from engineered defaults. Not just aspiring to presence, but making it easier. Not merely limiting screen time, but embedding rituals that naturally enforce it. Discipline gives way to design.

Readers will find practical strategies, certainly—but more importantly, a framework: habit as iterative identity refinement. What you do repeatedly becomes what you trust yourself to do. In a world engineered to fracture focus, consistency is an act of resistance. Mindful rituals restore that consistency. They are modest acts of defiance against digital drift, eventually forming the architecture of a life well-directed.

## The Power of Rituals Over Resolutions

A remarkable paradox shapes human behaviour: the more ambitious the resolution, the less likely it is to succeed. Despite widespread enthusiasm for personal transformation—fuelled by New Year declarations, digital detox challenges, or bold promises of a "new you"—most resolutions collapse under their own weight. Research consistently shows that over 80 percent of resolutions fail by February. The problem is not motivation, nor intelligence, nor even sincerity. The problem is structure. *Resolutions depend on bursts of effort; rituals rely on the gravity of repetition.* One is fuelled by inspiration; the other is anchored by design.

Daily rituals succeed where resolutions fail because they reduce reliance on willpower. Willpower is a finite resource. It is depleted by decision fatigue, emotional stress, and environmental friction. Resolutions—by their nature—assume a future self who will be perpetually motivated and perpetually rational. But no such self exists. What does exist is a present self who needs scaffolding—behavioural cues, time-bound repetition, and environmental support. *Rituals do not ask for heroic choices; they ask for consistent ones.* This is why they endure.

Consider the failure rate of digital detox commitments. A person declares, with genuine resolve, that they will "check their phone less" or "spend more time offline." The desire is clear. The intention is sound. But the execution is vague. When do they check their phone? What replaces that behaviour? What context triggers the habit? Without answers to these questions, the resolution has no grip. The moment of decision becomes a moment of friction, and friction is where good intentions often die. Rituals solve this not by intensifying motivation, but by eliminating ambiguity.

For example, a person who decides to "spend less time on social media" may delete an app out of frustration, only to reinstall it two days later. But a person who builds a ritual—placing their phone in a drawer after dinner, reading one printed article before bed, or using a physical notebook to plan the day—gradually shifts the environment and expectation. Over time, this ritual becomes self-reinforcing. It is not a moment of virtue. It is a normalised behaviour.

The strength of rituals lies in their relationship with identity. *What we do repeatedly becomes what we believe about ourselves.* A resolution often frames the self as broken—"I need to fix this"—whereas a ritual frames the self as evolving—"This is what I do." This distinction has psychological weight. Studies in behavioural psychology, including those led by James Clear and Charles Duhigg, confirm that identity-based habits are far more likely to stick. A person who sees themselves as "someone who doesn't scroll in the morning" acts in accordance with that self-image. They do not debate it daily. It is simply who they are.

Moreover, rituals allow for failure without collapse. One skipped day does not invalidate the identity or the habit. In contrast, resolutions often operate in binary terms—success or failure. This rigidity leads to a brittle psychology. The moment a resolution is broken, the entire effort is often abandoned. Rituals are more flexible. They expect imperfection. They thrive not in the absence of error, but in the presence of continuity. The phrase "I missed a day, but I'll return tomorrow" is central to their resilience.

Another crucial difference is the granularity of action. Resolutions are typically large in scope: "Be more present," "Use screens less," "Manage time better." They sound noble, but they lack behavioural resolution. Rituals work because they break large ambitions into small, repeatable acts: "After breakfast, I journal for five minutes without checking email"; "Every Sunday evening, I plan three offline blocks for the week"; "When I feel overwhelmed, I close my laptop and take one breath before opening another tab." These rituals may appear trivial, but *they generate behavioural momentum.* The cumulative effect of small, deliberate actions far outweighs the occasional grand gesture.

This is particularly relevant in the context of technology, where frictionless design invites frictionless consumption. The digital world is engineered to bypass deliberation. Infinite scroll, autoplay, notifications—all are built to erode intentionality. The antidote is not more willpower. It is more structure. Rituals introduce friction *where it matters most*: at the entry point of distraction. They create pre-commitment points—tiny pauses, environmental shifts, or symbolic actions—that reset the user's posture toward technology. A ritualised phone handover at dinner, for instance, changes the social tone of a meal. A designated "off-switch" song before bed transforms sleep preparation into a sensory cue. These are not resolutions. They are anchors.

It is also important to recognise that rituals are not merely behavioural—they are temporal. They shape the rhythm of life. Morning routines, weekly reviews, monthly resets—these are temporal rituals that restore coherence in an otherwise fragmented attention economy. In the absence of such rituals, the day becomes reactive. The device dictates the rhythm. Notifications replace reflection. Time blurs. Attention frays. But when certain times of day or week are *reserved*, when particular actions always happen in those slots, time regains form. *Rituals reassert authorship over time.*

Sociologically, rituals also carry symbolic value. They are shared cues of meaning. Religious rituals, meal blessings, sabbath days, and even pre-performance routines in sports serve not only practical functions but *cognitive orientation*. They signal identity, intention, and transition. In modern secular life, especially amid digital saturation, these rituals have eroded—but the need for them has not. The rise of digital Sabbath movements, phone-free zones, and device check-in rituals at family gatherings reflects a cultural hunger for symbolic structure. These behaviours succeed not because they are enforced, but because they are *felt*. They create space, both physically and mentally.

It is worth noting that not all rituals are beneficial. Many are maladaptive. Checking email before getting out of bed, scrolling during meals, watching YouTube before sleep—these, too, are rituals. They are rituals of drift. They form unintentionally, but they follow the same principles of repetition and environmental cueing. The difference is that they erode intentionality rather than reinforcing it. The solution is not to eliminate rituals, but to *replace unconscious rituals with deliberate ones*. You cannot destroy a cue-response loop. You can only rewrite it.

Philosophically, this invites a broader question: *What kind of life are you rehearsing through your rituals?* Every repeated action is a rehearsal for identity. The person who meditates each morning, not because they feel like it but because they do it regardless of feeling, is rehearsing attention. The person who turns off their phone for 30 minutes at lunch is rehearsing presence. These rituals may be private, but their effects are public. They shape mood, focus, and interaction. They are the invisible architecture of a well-directed life.

To implement rituals that stick, the essential ingredients are specificity, simplicity, and salience. A good ritual is clearly defined ("at 8am, I do X"), easy to execute (it requires no elaborate setup), and emotionally resonant (it reminds you why it matters). When rituals meet these criteria, they become sticky. They fit the contours of your life. They are not tasks to remember. They are acts you return to.

And most critically, *they don't ask you to become someone else overnight.* They allow you to *become yourself on purpose.* Not by declaration, but by repetition. Not through pressure, but through presence. In this way, rituals are the antidote to both overwhelm and inertia. They offer a form of behavioural sovereignty that resolutions, for all their passion, simply cannot provide.

In a culture that rewards spectacle and short bursts of effort, the quiet repetition of a personal ritual may seem insignificant. But over time, it becomes the foundation of autonomy. Not just what you do, but who you are becoming. And that—far more than any fleeting resolution—is what endures.

## One Habit at a Time

Most people fail to change their behaviour not because they lack motivation, but because they attempt too much, too quickly, with too little structure. The assumption is that if one habit is good, five are better. This mentality—rooted in ambition rather than understanding—leads to an overloaded will, brittle routines, and inevitable backsliding. Yet behaviour change, when designed effectively, does not require radical transformation. It requires frictionless initiation, precise anchoring, and consistent repetition. *The principle is simple but powerful: one habit at a time, anchored to what already works.*

This is the logic behind micro-habit stacking—a behavioural approach grounded in the realities of human attention, emotional bandwidth, and neural adaptation. Rather than building new routines from scratch, habit stacking attaches a new micro-behaviour to an existing stable routine. The brain loves patterns. It resists disruption. Habit stacking leverages this neurological preference by *embedding new habits into old ones*, thereby reducing cognitive load and increasing behavioural stability.

Take, for example, the simple but profound difference between deciding to "reduce screen time in the evenings" versus adding a specific, stacked behaviour: "After brushing my teeth, I will place my phone in the kitchen and plug it in." The first is abstract and intention-based. The second is concrete and behaviour-based. It attaches the new habit (putting the phone away) to an established anchor (brushing teeth), thus removing decision fatigue from the equation. Over time, the stacked habit becomes automatic because the brain anticipates it as part of a sequence.

This methodology draws from several converging strands of behavioural science. Research by BJ Fogg at Stanford University, for instance, emphasises the power of *tiny habits*—behaviours so small they are nearly frictionless. When paired with a clear anchor (such as "after I make coffee" or "after I shut down my laptop"), these micro-habits gain momentum without requiring dramatic motivation. Similarly, Charles Duhigg's cue-routine-reward model illustrates how new behaviours can ride the coattails of old routines by repurposing existing cues. *The stacking of one deliberate behaviour onto another is not a motivational hack; it is a structural upgrade to how habits are formed.*

Critically, micro-habit stacking works not because the behaviours are easy, but because the activation energy is low. The hardest part of any action is starting. Once a person begins, even the smallest motion, they are far more likely to continue. A person who commits to "read one paragraph of a book after making tea" often ends up reading a chapter. A person who "sits quietly for thirty seconds after turning off their alarm" often ends up meditating for five minutes. But these outcomes are not the target. The target is consistency. *The beauty of micro-habit stacking is that success is measured by initiation, not completion.*

This distinction matters in a culture obsessed with outcomes. Most people abandon habits because they don't see fast results. But habits are not goals; they are systems. Their power compounds slowly, invisibly, and then unmistakably. In the early days of habit change, it is the *installation* of the behaviour—not its impact—that matters most. Micro-habit stacking ensures that the installation process is frictionless enough to repeat, yet structured enough to endure.

When applied to digital behaviour, this technique is particularly effective because it replaces vague aspirations with specific protocols. Rather than resolving to "be less distracted," one might stack a habit like "After opening my laptop, I will open a blank document before checking email." Rather than hoping to "be more present at dinner," one might stack "After placing the plates on the table, I will power off my phone and put it in a drawer." These micro-actions, repeated daily, become habits not through intensity, but through rhythm.

The psychological power of habit stacking also lies in its momentum effect. A small win, consistently repeated, builds self-efficacy—the belief that change is possible. This matters enormously. Most behaviour change falters not due to lack of skill or strategy, but because the person doesn't believe they are the kind of person who follows through. Every successful micro-habit is a behavioural vote cast for a new identity. Over time, the person no longer says "I want to be less reactive online"; they say, "I'm someone who creates space before responding." That shift in identity reinforces the habit, and the habit reinforces the identity. *Change becomes a loop, not a leap.*

Of course, there are limitations to the stacking method, and understanding these boundaries is part of intelligent application. Not every behaviour can be miniaturised. Not every cue is suitable for anchoring. And not every habit can be layered at once. This is why the "one habit at a time" principle matters. Cognitive bandwidth is finite. Emotional bandwidth even more so. When people attempt to stack multiple habits in parallel—changing morning, evening, and work routines simultaneously—they dilute attention, introduce conflict between behaviours, and risk destabilising the system. The most sustainable habit architectures are *incremental by design*. They allow for phase-based growth.

There is also the question of timing. When is a habit ready to be stacked? The answer is when the previous habit is *automatic*. This is a test of behavioural fluency. If a person no longer has to think about performing the anchor habit, if it happens almost reflexively, then that cue is stable enough to carry another behaviour. Premature stacking creates instability. Effective stacking requires patience. One habit, solidified. Then another, layered. Like bricks, each one must be level before the next is placed.

Environmental design plays a complementary role here. Habit stacking works best when supported by environmental cues—objects, layouts, or contexts that reinforce the action. For example, leaving a journal open on the desk next to the coffee mug increases the likelihood that the "after coffee, I journal one sentence" habit will occur. Likewise, placing a physical book on the pillow each morning reinforces the evening habit of reading before sleep. *Environment is not just background; it is scaffolding.* And when the physical environment reinforces the stacked habits, behavioural stability increases dramatically.

Importantly, micro-habit stacking should not be confused with triviality. These are not token gestures or productivity theatre. They are intentional rehearsals of behavioural patterns that compound over time. A two-minute mindfulness pause, anchored to the act of logging into a device, might sound insignificant. But if repeated daily, it shifts the user's digital posture from reactive to reflective. A single sentence of handwritten journaling might appear minimal. But over months, it becomes a record of values, moods, and thought patterns. *These small actions, when structured well, become rituals of intentionality.*

Nor should this method be viewed as a shortcut. It is not about "tricking" the brain. It is about aligning with the way behaviour actually works—through repetition, environmental cueing, and emotional reinforcement. The appeal of micro-habit stacking is not that it avoids effort, but that it applies effort precisely. Like compound interest, the return is slow at first, then exponential. It rewards those who persist beyond the novelty.

As with all behaviour change frameworks, context and reflection matter. What works for one person's attention span, schedule, or values may not work for another. The key is *personal congruence*. The stacked habits must fit the person's life—not in theory, but in practice. This requires experimentation. Some anchor cues may be too unstable. Some micro-behaviours may be too disruptive. Iteration is not failure; it is how sustainable systems are built. The person who refines their stack three times before it clicks has not delayed success—they have built the conditions for it.

In the end, micro-habit stacking is not just a productivity technique. It is a philosophy of change rooted in humility and intelligence. It acknowledges that our will is not infinite, that our time is not elastic, and that our attention must be directed with care. It builds a life not through aspiration, but through architecture. And it does so *one habit at a time.*

## Building Keystone Habits

Not all habits are created equal. Some serve a single purpose, modestly enhancing a routine. Others exert disproportionate influence over multiple domains of life, triggering a chain reaction of positive change. These are known as keystone habits—a term popularised in behavioural science and organisational psychology, denoting patterns of behaviour that, once established, catalyse improvement in seemingly unrelated areas. *Keystone habits are not merely habits; they are levers. They create structural integrity for change.*

The concept traces its origins to studies on habit loops and identity formation, but gained prominence through Charles Duhigg's influential work, which documented how keystone habits shape everything from individual productivity to institutional culture. For instance, research on individuals who begin regular exercise shows an increase not only in physical health, but also in dietary choices, sleep patterns, time management, even financial discipline. The act of exercising—a single behaviour—generates a ripple effect because it *alters the self-perception of the person performing it.* They begin to see themselves as disciplined, proactive, capable. This identity shift recalibrates future choices across multiple spheres.

But the power of keystone habits extends beyond their symbolic resonance. What distinguishes them functionally is that they *reorganise other behaviours around them.* They restructure priorities, create natural routines, and change how people allocate attention and emotional energy. Consider the example of consistent morning journaling. At face value, this may appear as a reflective exercise. But for many, it becomes the organisational centre of the day—a moment of cognitive clearing that reduces emotional reactivity, increases clarity of goals, and subtly strengthens impulse control. The habit doesn't stay confined to the page. It governs the next decision, and the next.

This cascading influence is the signature of a keystone habit: it produces second-order effects that exceed its first-order intention. It also typically exhibits three shared traits. First, it reshapes identity. Second, it introduces a sense of momentum or structure. Third, it offers cognitive or emotional returns that reinforce its recurrence. These traits make keystone habits not only effective, but *sticky*. They are more likely to endure because they are rewarded across multiple dimensions—functionally, emotionally, and symbolically.

From a psychological perspective, the efficacy of keystone habits lies in their ability to reduce cognitive friction. The human brain seeks pattern and efficiency. When one action organises others—when it becomes the *organising principle* of a routine—the brain expends less effort navigating daily life. This is why, in the context of digital habits, certain keystone behaviours are especially powerful. For example, a daily "digital shutdown" ritual in the evening—turning off all screens at a fixed hour—can improve sleep hygiene, enhance evening presence, and lead to lower stress the next day. One habit, multiple domains affected.

The challenge lies not in recognising that keystone habits exist, but in *identifying which ones matter most for the individual.* Keystone status is contextual. What becomes transformative for one person may be irrelevant to another. For a chronically distracted professional, a keystone habit may be a structured morning without phone access. For a person navigating emotional overwhelm, it may be a five-minute breathwork practice. For someone recovering from tech overuse, it may be the simple but consistent action of logging off all apps after a fixed time. *The power of a keystone habit is measured not by its intensity, but by its strategic placement within the architecture of a person's life.*

There is also a deeper behavioural logic to consider. Keystone habits succeed because they often influence *how people make decisions*, not just *which decisions they make*. Take the habit of meal planning on Sunday evenings. On the surface, this affects food choices. But its deeper function is that it reduces decision fatigue throughout the week, frees cognitive bandwidth, and creates temporal boundaries that discourage impulsive scrolling during mealtimes. The habit is nutritional, yes—but it is also attentional, emotional, and logistical.

This kind of spillover effect makes keystone habits especially relevant in an era of fragmented attention. Digital environments, designed to hijack focus and reward impulse, erode the very conditions that support deep habits. In response, keystone habits can serve as *anchors*—points of stability in an otherwise volatile landscape. A consistent early-morning routine that includes ten minutes of movement, three minutes of stillness, and one minute of intention-setting might sound modest. But over months, it creates a structural counterbalance to the entropy of digital life. It becomes the architecture of intentionality.

Crucially, keystone habits do not require elaborate systems or extreme willpower. In fact, they often succeed precisely because they are *friction-sensitive.* They adapt to the person's environment, energy levels, and psychological readiness. This is why starting small is not a weakness, but a strategic strength. A keystone habit that starts as "write one line in a journal" can scale over time into a sophisticated reflective practice. But its effectiveness depends on reliability, not intensity. *What makes a keystone habit powerful is not how hard it is, but how consistently it happens.*

Still, this raises an important question: how can individuals identify their own keystone habits amid the noise of competing priorities?

One approach is to examine patterns retrospectively. Which behaviours, when they occur, lead to a disproportionately better day? Which routines, even when brief, restore clarity, reduce reactivity, or create order? These are often clues. Another approach is to experiment with *meta-habits*—habits that direct attention toward other habits. For instance, a weekly reflection practice where one evaluates which behaviours felt centring, which felt draining, can reveal powerful insight. The keystone habit may not always be the most visible—it is often the *quiet rhythm* behind other sustainable patterns.

It is also essential to differentiate between aspirational habits and structural habits. Aspirational habits are those we *want* to have—meditation, exercise, digital detoxing—but which often remain inconsistent because they lack anchoring. Structural habits, by contrast, are those that stabilise other actions, even if they are less glamorous. For instance, going to sleep and waking at consistent times may not seem life-changing, but this rhythm can cascade into better focus, reduced cravings, and more resilient emotional regulation. Structural habits tend to become keystones not because they're aspirational, but because they're *foundational.* They make other behaviours more likely to occur.

The key, ultimately, is *selective focus.* Trying to build ten good habits in parallel creates noise, dilution, and fatigue. But building one carefully chosen keystone habit—one that aligns with values, reinforces identity, and influences multiple domains—creates clarity. It narrows the behavioural aperture, making follow-through more likely. It turns habit-building into a precision craft, not a motivational gamble.

This is particularly important for those seeking to redesign their digital lives. The temptation is often to implement sweeping reforms: block all social media, install productivity apps, overhaul routines. But such overhauls rarely last. What does last is one keystone behaviour that shifts the relationship to digital environments. For example, a commitment to "no phone use during the first hour after waking" might recalibrate the day's emotional tone, protect mental bandwidth, and reduce downstream scrolling. That one action, if ritualised, becomes the stabilising axis around which healthier behaviours rotate.

As in architecture, so in habit design: *the integrity of the structure depends on the placement of the keystone.* Done well, it supports everything around it. Done poorly—or chosen without care—it leaves the system unstable. The person trying to build a more intentional, less distracted life must ask not just "What habits do I want?" but "What habits will support everything else I value?" Keystone habits answer this question not through complexity, but through leverage. They are not additive; they are multiplicative.

Behaviour change is not a project. It is a practice. And like all effective practices, it requires focus, sequencing, and intelligent design. Keystone habits embody all three. They offer an elegant path forward—simple, strategic, and stabilising. For those willing to build carefully, *they become the hidden architecture of a life well lived.*

## Tracking, Not Policing

It is often said that what gets measured gets managed. But in the domain of personal habits—particularly those involving technology and attention—measurement is not a neutral act. The way we track our behaviours can either foster awareness and growth, or slide into obsessive micromanagement that constricts rather than empowers. *The core challenge is this: how do we observe our digital patterns with clarity, without turning self-awareness into self-surveillance?* In a culture saturated with metrics, dashboards, and quantified selves, the answer is neither more tracking nor none at all. It is *better tracking*—light-touch, humane, and oriented toward insight rather than control.

Modern behavioural science has firmly established that self-monitoring can improve outcomes across domains, from physical health to time use. But the effect is not universally positive. Context, intention, and method matter. Studies on wearable fitness devices, for example, reveal mixed results. For some users, step counts and heart rate data encourage healthier decisions. For others, the same metrics induce anxiety, undermine intrinsic motivation, or foster compulsive checking. The difference is not in the data, but in the *relationship to the data.* When tracking becomes a proxy for self-worth, or when it amplifies guilt without offering agency, it ceases to be a tool and becomes a leash.

In the digital space, this tension is particularly acute. Many people intuitively feel their screen time is excessive or misaligned with their values. But when presented with raw usage data—from apps like Screen Time, RescueTime, or Digital Wellbeing—the result is often not constructive reflection but defensiveness, shame, or fatigue. This is because most tracking tools adopt a *surveillance frame*, implicitly judging time as "productive" or "wasted," rather than *curious observation*, which would invite open-ended exploration of patterns and trade-offs. The difference between the two is subtle but foundational. *Surveillance asks, "Did I do enough?"; curiosity asks, "What happened, and why?"*

To cultivate mindful digital habits, then, the goal is not to reject tracking altogether, but to design *gentle tracking systems* that support self-understanding without becoming a psychological burden. This begins with reframing the purpose of tracking. The objective is not accountability to an external standard, but alignment with internal priorities. Are the behaviours I'm engaging in reflective of the life I want to live? Does my digital time serve or subvert my deeper goals? These questions cannot be answered by numbers alone. But numbers, selectively used, can illuminate blind spots that subjective reflection may miss.

Consider the case of a knowledge worker who wants to reduce reactive email checking. Rather than installing rigid blocks or punitive timers, they simply track *email opens per hour* over a typical week, without judgment. The data shows a spike in the late afternoon—a time when energy is low and task-switching feels like relief. This insight suggests not a discipline failure, but a pattern linked to circadian rhythm and task fatigue. The intervention that follows is not harder rules, but smarter design: bundling all email replies into a 4:00pm block, and inserting a short walk or tea break before it. *Tracking here functions not as discipline enforcement, but as pattern detection. It reveals causes, not just symptoms.*

Another example lies in the habit of nightly scrolling before bed. Many users wish to reduce this behaviour, citing poor sleep or morning grogginess. Instead of tracking screen time in total, which is diffuse and overwhelming, a more effective approach is to track *what triggers the scroll.* Is it boredom, loneliness, procrastination, or overstimulation from the day? Keeping a brief nightly note—just a few words capturing context—can create a narrative pattern over time. This is a form of *qualitative tracking*, which is often more illuminating than quantitative metrics. It invites reflection and compassion, rather than judgment and correction.

Importantly, light-touch tracking also respects the limitations of human attention. Any system that requires constant input or elaborate categorisation is unlikely to be sustained. Minimalist tracking strategies—such as binary yes/no logs, quick ratings (e.g., "focus quality: 1–5"), or once-weekly reviews—tend to perform better in the long run. They lower the cognitive overhead of tracking itself, allowing it to remain a means, not an end. And they prevent the subtle trap of *tracking as procrastination*, in which the act of monitoring becomes a substitute for change.

But even minimalist tracking must be held in the right psychological posture. The key is *non-identification*—remembering that tracked data is not the self, but a reflection of temporary conditions. This distinction is critical. People who track their focus and find it "poor" three days in a row may be tempted to internalise a negative narrative: *I'm broken, undisciplined, failing.* But if the same data is held as *contextual*—perhaps due to stress, illness, or poor sleep—the story changes. The tracking becomes an opportunity to adjust the system, not blame the person. This is how tracking supports growth: *by offering feedback, not indictment.*

There is also a philosophical question underneath all of this: What kind of relationship do we want with ourselves? The language of "optimisation," so common in tech and productivity circles, implies that the human is a machine to be tuned, a problem to be solved. But humans are not spreadsheets. Our behaviours are embedded in emotion, history, culture, and environment. To track well is to honour this complexity—not reduce it to bar charts and averages. It is to say, *I want to understand myself, not fix myself.* This subtle shift reframes the entire enterprise of self-monitoring.

Of course, there are moments when more structured tracking is appropriate—especially during habit formation. But even here, it is the tone that matters. A person trying to reduce compulsive social media use might use a calendar to mark "clean" days. The key is not the mark, but what it represents. If it becomes a badge of moral worth, a source of anxiety when broken, it backfires. But if it is used as a visual cue, a prompt to celebrate progress and recommit after lapses, it can be highly effective. *The best tracking systems are compassionate systems.*

The future of digital self-regulation may well depend on this shift—from data-driven policing to pattern-oriented noticing. As more people seek to reclaim their time, attention, and peace from hyperstimulating technologies, tracking must evolve. It must become less about extraction and more about insight. Less about metrics and more about meaning. This requires a different kind of design—one rooted in *respect for the user's humanity*. App developers, too, must take note. Tools that prompt reflection without judgment, that surface trends without triggering anxiety, will define the next generation of mindful tech.

Ultimately, tracking is only as good as the questions it invites. Not "how many hours did I waste?" but "what does this pattern tell me about what I need?" Not "am I good or bad today?" but "how can I meet myself where I am, and go forward from here?" The moment tracking becomes a stick rather than a compass, it loses its power. But when designed with intelligence and used with grace, it becomes a mirror—not harsh, but honest. Not punitive, but perceptive.

In a world eager to digitise everything, the temptation is always toward more measurement, more quantification, more data. But the wisdom lies not in how much we track, but *how we relate to what we notice*. Light-touch tracking offers a middle path—one that balances rigour with kindness, and accountability with autonomy. It doesn't promise perfection. But it promises something better: *a way to see clearly, choose wisely, and change gently*.

# Chapter 8
# Redesigning Your Digital Spaces

Most people underestimate just how profoundly their environment shapes behaviour. They might notice that a cluttered kitchen makes healthy eating more difficult, or that a tidy desk improves concentration. Yet when it comes to digital surroundings—the apps we open, the interfaces we navigate, the notifications that constantly tug at us—the same awareness is often missing. Digital environments may feel weightless and intangible, but they are far from neutral. They are deliberately constructed, engineered to capture attention, prompt reactions, and mould behaviour. And like any environment, they can be redesigned—strategically, thoughtfully, and in alignment with what truly matters.

Attention is not merely a matter of willpower. It responds to cues, triggers, and the ease—or friction—embedded within the systems around us. In this sense, digital spaces function as terrains, not simply tools. They can guide reflection or lure compulsive reactivity. A crowded home screen, a browser brimming with tabs, or an algorithm prioritising outrage over insight—these are not minor irritations. They are behavioural scripts, subtly determining what we notice, what we ignore, and how fully we engage with any task.

To navigate the digital age deliberately, we must learn to become architects of our own attention ecosystems. This chapter presents that practice—not as a productivity trick, but as a design ethic. The goal is not to renounce technology, nor to wage war on screens. It is to renegotiate our engagement, using environmental design to align digital spaces with our deeper intentions. Our phones, apps, desktops, and interfaces are not fixed givens; they are editable contexts. And left at default, they are optimised for purposes other than our own.

Consider the smartphone home screen. Users unlock their phones dozens of times a day, often without any specific reason. Why? Because the interface is designed like a slot machine—rows of vibrant icons, red badges, instant access to every potential distraction. This is rarely a matter of weakness; it is environmental engineering. Simply moving high-distraction apps off the home screen—or uninstalling them entirely—introduces a small amount of friction, enough to reinsert intentionality. Over time, such tweaks shift behaviour from reactive to reflective.

Friction, properly applied, becomes a feature rather than a bug. Modern design often seeks to eliminate it, smoothing every interaction. Yet, in digital wellbeing, friction can serve as a gentle prompt: a password to enter social media, a greyscale screen in the evening, website blockers that pause rather than forbid. These interventions add a second for reflection before the click—a pause that radically changes engagement in an age of instant access.

Workspaces demand the same attention. A laptop littered with tabs, notifications, and bookmarks to dopamine-heavy sites quietly undermines depth of thought. A digital desktop, like a physical one, benefits from minimalism, zoning, and purposeful cues. Grouping work apps together, using a clean wallpaper, enabling full-screen modes—these are not purely aesthetic choices. They are cognitive scaffolds, shaping not only what we do, but how we think while doing it. Interface clarity translates directly into mental clarity.

Beyond layout, intentional zoning adds another layer. Just as a home has rooms for rest, work, or conversation, digital zones can reflect modes of mind. A "deep work" space might include writing tools, research materials, and ambient music, with distractions filtered. A "social" zone could confine messaging apps to set hours. A "rest" zone might contain podcasts, reading apps, or mindfulness tools—curated to restore rather than overstimulate. This is not about rigidity, but about signalling context. When devices communicate their purpose, they become partners in focus rather than agents of fragmentation.

This shift—from default to deliberate—invites a larger reimagining. What if our devices were not just escape valves but intentional spaces? Many of us reach for phones to soothe or distract, chasing fleeting dopamine hits. But a small redesign can transform the impulse: open a journaling app instead of Instagram, a blank writing canvas instead of a newsfeed, a breathing exercise instead of a weather report. Tiny interventions, repeated, move interaction from passive consumption to deliberate engagement.

There is a deeper philosophical dimension. Environmental cues, once internalised, shape character. Digital environments do more than guide behaviour; they sculpt identity. A cluttered digital landscape fosters reactivity, just as a messy home reflects a scattered mind. Redesigning these spaces is an act of self-authorship. It declares: I will not be shaped by defaults; I will shape my context to reflect my values.

This is not a call for perfectionism, nor a critique of technology itself. It is an invitation to engage with tools thoughtfully, intentionally, and humanely. Digital decluttering is not asceticism—it is reclaiming choice. Friction signals pause and awareness. Zones invite depth. And what once served as escape can become exploration.

By the chapter's end, readers will acquire practical strategies for reshaping their digital spaces, but more importantly, a new perspective: environments are never neutral. Every design choice—however small—expresses care. As an architect considers how a room will feel to its inhabitants, so can we design our digital world for clarity, presence, and meaningful engagement. This is not a technical exercise—it is philosophical. And it begins wherever you are, one icon, one layout, one intentional moment of attention at a time.

## Decluttering the Digital Environment

The human brain evolved to make sense of its environment through structure, rhythm, and spatial clarity. In physical space, we instinctively understand the difference between a tidy room and a chaotic one. We know the unease of piles of unopened mail, cluttered countertops, and overflowing drawers—not just for the inconvenience they bring, but for the cognitive drag they impose. What we are slower to grasp, however, is that our *digital environments*—invisible, persistent, and largely unexamined—carry similar weight. Every open tab, every red notification badge, every bloated desktop or cluttered app drawer becomes a form of digital noise. Not because it shouts audibly, but because it silently siphons attention. *Aesthetics shape cognition. Layout informs intention. Visual order, or its absence, has real consequences for how we think, feel, and act.*

While minimalism in interior design has been explored and embraced for decades, its digital analogue is still catching up. Most people accept the default visual and spatial setup of their devices without questioning its impact. But these defaults are rarely neutral. They reflect the priorities of developers, not the mental well-being of users. The result is a paradox: our physical spaces may be designed with intention, while our digital ones—where we now spend the majority of our waking hours—are often left uncurated. And yet it is these digital spaces that act as launchpads for decisions, reflections, connections, and distractions. Their influence is not peripheral—it is central. *Decluttering the digital environment is not about cosmetic minimalism; it is about reclaiming cognitive agency.*

A phone screen with five rows of apps, each bristling with colour-coded icons and badges, is not merely a neutral utility. It is a behavioural script. It tells the brain that everything is equally urgent, equally relevant, equally deserving of a tap. It dissolves hierarchy and invites compulsive checking. The same applies to browser tabs. A user with eighteen tabs open is, neurologically speaking, standing at the intersection of eighteen unfinished thoughts. The brain, which craves closure and clarity, is kept in a constant state of low-grade tension. The unfinished tabs whisper from the background, taxing working memory even when not actively in use. The burden is subtle, but persistent. *Mental clutter is often architectural before it is emotional.*

Decluttering, then, is not an act of denial but of design. It begins with recognising that the visual landscape of your screen determines your perceptual priorities. When everything is present, nothing stands out. When everything is accessible, nothing feels intentional. A cleaner interface doesn't just look better—it *works better.* It provides cognitive breathing room. Consider the difference between an inbox with 12,000 unread messages and one with zero. Functionally, both can be used to send and receive emails. But one promotes paralysis; the other promotes engagement. That difference is not technical—it is psychological.

Design researchers and interface psychologists have long understood this. The concept of "affordances"—the design elements that suggest their own use—means that cluttered, unstructured environments do not merely offer options; they *invite distractions.* A carousel of icons says: tap something, anything. A cascade of open windows says: keep toggling. Designers of attention-maximising platforms exploit this reality. But it can be harnessed differently. A clean digital desktop with only two or three key tools says: here's where to focus. A phone with only essential utilities on the home screen says: this device is not a toy chest.

Real-world case studies reinforce the power of layout as behavioural architecture. In workplaces where digital dashboards were simplified—removing redundant analytics, hiding non-essential data, and colour-coding critical fields—employees consistently reported less decision fatigue and improved focus. In classrooms where students' tablets were preloaded with only the day's required tools, time-on-task increased significantly. These are not anecdotes about aesthetics; they are demonstrations of how spatial logic alters mental clarity. *Form is never separate from function in environments of use.*

This applies as much to individuals as to institutions. Personal devices, especially, benefit from periodic digital audits. Just as a wardrobe accumulates items no longer worn, a phone accumulates apps no longer needed. The unused fitness tracker, the game you stopped playing months ago, the expired shopping app—all of these remain as low-level cognitive noise. Deleting them doesn't just free storage space; it *frees attentional space.* A sparse environment demands less triage. It reduces the number of micro-decisions we make each day, which—when added up—can be surprisingly depleting.

Importantly, decluttering is not a single act but a recurring discipline. It parallels physical tidying: you don't vacuum once and declare your floors permanently clean. It requires weekly or monthly sweeps, mindful maintenance, and above all, a clear understanding of *what the space is for.* Is your laptop a creative workspace, a communication hub, or a casual browsing tool? Different functions warrant different designs. A writing-focused setup benefits from full-screen modes, quiet backgrounds, and minimal dock icons. A communication-focused setup may embrace faster switching between chat platforms but hide social feeds. The key is not uniformity, but *purpose-aligned design.*

There are psychological gains to be made as well. Digital clutter correlates with decision fatigue and emotional volatility. In contrast, visual order promotes calm and self-efficacy. This isn't merely about feeling better—it's about performing better. When your device is configured to reflect your actual priorities, it becomes an ally rather than an adversary. You open it not into a marketplace of random urges, but into a sanctuary of considered intention. *That shift changes not just what you do, but how you do it.*

There are counterarguments worth considering. Some may argue that clutter is a sign of creativity—that a messy desktop reflects a fertile mind. And yes, for certain temperaments, chaos *can* serve as fuel. But even in these cases, clutter must be *curated*, not accidental. There is a difference between a collage and a dump. Between layered inputs and random noise. The question is not whether the environment is spare or rich—it is whether it is *designed.* Default clutter is not creativity. It is inertia.

Moreover, aesthetics matter beyond function. The visual feel of a space—digital or otherwise—shapes our emotional tone. A beautifully arranged digital workspace invites reverence, even care. It signals that the work being done within it is valuable. Conversely, a chaotic, broken interface subtly signals that what happens here is disposable. People often underestimate the *moral dimension* of design—the way in which our spaces influence not only what we do, but *what we believe about the doing.* Decluttering, then, is an act of valuing our time, our focus, and our inner life.

In a world saturated with designed distraction, reclaiming our digital environment is not indulgence—it is resistance. It is an insistence that our tools reflect our values, not just our impulses. It is an acknowledgement that *attention is shaped by what surrounds it*, and that those surroundings can, and must, be crafted with care. The next time you open your device, ask not just what you want to do—but whether the space invites that doing. If not, redesign it. The costs of chaos are subtle but cumulative. The gains of clarity, once felt, are hard to forget.

This is where the true value of digital decluttering lies—not in minimalism for its own sake, but in recovering a sense of *cognitive sovereignty*. It is a statement of intent: *I will not let my environment shape me by default. I will shape it to serve my best work, clearest thinking, and deepest attention.* That is not merely a matter of productivity. It is a matter of dignity.

## Friction as a Feature

One of the great design mantras of the digital age is "frictionless experience." It's repeated in design sprints, product reviews, and UX workshops like gospel. The assumption behind it seems harmless, even benevolent: people want speed, simplicity, and immediacy—so the job of good design is to remove all barriers between intent and action. Clicks should be minimised, interfaces should be intuitive, and access should be instantaneous. But this unquestioned pursuit of ease conceals a deeper problem: when it comes to digital habits, *what's frictionless is not always harmless*. In fact, the very smoothness that defines modern technology often accelerates behaviours we'd prefer to limit—scrolling, checking, bingeing, reacting—without ever asking us to notice we're doing them.

Friction is not the enemy of good design. *Misplaced friction is*. Waiting two minutes for a web page to load is bad friction. Requiring five different forms to access a simple service is bad friction. But thoughtfully *placed* friction—deliberate speed bumps that slow us down at crucial decision points—can be profoundly beneficial. This is especially true in the context of screen-related behaviours that thrive on automaticity. The more seamless the path to distraction, the more likely we are to take it. The more delayed the impulse, the more likely we are to reconsider. The key insight is this: *friction, when applied intentionally, can be a tool of self-direction rather than an obstacle to usability*.

Consider the now-ubiquitous practice of infinite scrolling. There is no endpoint. No signal that one has reached the bottom of the page. No prompt to pause. It is designed to remove all natural stopping cues, so the user keeps going—not because they choose to, but because there is no moment to opt out. Friction, in this context, would mean the opposite: introducing natural breaks in content, placing prompts to reflect, or requiring some form of user input to continue. A page that stops after 20 entries and asks, "Want to see more?" is not impeding you; it's *returning your agency*. It creates a micro-moment in which awareness can re-enter the loop.

Research in behavioural economics consistently shows that people are far more influenced by *default settings* than they realise. If a choice is made easy, we are more likely to go with it—whether that choice involves donating organs, joining a mailing list, or opening social media the moment we wake up. But the same research also shows that *minor obstacles* can dramatically reduce unwanted behaviour. For example, studies have found that placing sweets in opaque jars instead of transparent ones significantly reduces workplace snacking. The difference isn't willpower—it's visibility and access. In digital contexts, this translates to features like requiring a password to open social media apps, disabling automatic login, or placing apps in folders that require an extra swipe to access. These are not tricks or hacks. They are *design interventions* that leverage friction as intentional feedback.

The principle extends well beyond devices. In environments where friction has been strategically reintroduced, people tend to make more deliberate choices. One compelling example comes from libraries that restructured their digital catalogues to include a "Do You Really Need to Print This?" prompt before completing a print job. Printing volumes dropped by over 30%. Not because anyone was banned from printing, but because the added prompt slowed down the process just enough to restore conscious reflection. This is the essence of productive friction: *it breaks the spell of momentum long enough to ask—Is this worth doing?*

Intentional friction is particularly relevant in moments where our behaviours are habitual and emotionally driven. Think of checking news apps during moments of anxiety, refreshing email compulsively when bored, or opening Instagram at the first hint of discomfort. These are not reflective acts; they are reactive ones. But small frictions—such as disabling notifications, removing badges, or logging out of the app—introduce just enough delay to allow the prefrontal cortex to re-engage. This shift, from impulsive to intentional, is often all it takes to change the course of action.

Critics may argue that adding friction is tantamount to paternalism—that it infantilises users by interfering with their choices. But this objection collapses under scrutiny. First, *we are already operating in an environment shaped by design decisions we did not make.* The current default—ease, immediacy, and endless novelty—is not neutral. It is the result of platforms maximising for engagement rather than well-being. Second, introducing friction does not remove choice—it restores it. It creates the conditions for conscious agency by slowing the loop between trigger and behaviour. *Friction is not a leash; it is a mirror.*

This reframing opens up new possibilities for personal and professional contexts. A writer, for example, may install software that locks access to the internet during work sessions—not to punish themselves, but to remove the possibility of mid-paragraph Googling spirals. A parent might set a ten-minute delay before a streaming app launches, making binge-watching feel just inconvenient enough to reconsider. A team leader might introduce a policy where meeting invites require a written agenda before being sent, reducing unnecessary calendar clutter. These are all examples of friction used not as restriction, but as design-based reflection prompts. They ask: *Are you sure this is the best use of your time?*

Philosophically, the idea of friction-as-feature challenges a deeper cultural narrative—that ease is always good, and difficulty always bad. But this is a child's logic. Adults understand that meaningful achievement often requires resistance. Muscles grow under strain. Skills deepen through repetition. Relationships mature through discomfort. The same applies to habits of mind. If attention is our most valuable resource—as argued throughout this book—then it deserves safeguards, not open pipelines. *Discomfort is not the enemy of freedom; distraction is.*

At a societal level, this reframing also has policy implications. Platforms that engineer away all barriers to consumption are not just efficient—they are exploitative. When YouTube auto-plays the next video without a pause, when TikTok loads new content in milliseconds, when social apps eliminate the need to search by feeding a tailored stream—the user is no longer choosing; they are being chosen for. Introducing friction in these contexts—be it through design legislation or interface regulation—is not a curtailment of liberty, but a protection of autonomy. *Real freedom requires time to think, and friction creates that time.*

None of this is to suggest that all technology should be made harder to use. Many systems—medical databases, emergency services, educational platforms—depend on speed and efficiency. Friction should not be indiscriminate. It should be *situated*—applied where behavioural momentum outpaces reflection. In these spaces, small obstacles serve as cognitive ramps, lifting behaviour out of the basement of impulse and into the penthouse of intention.

For individuals, the invitation is clear: design your tools to *ask before acting*. Introduce just enough effort to turn automatic habits into conscious ones. Whether that means moving your email app to the second screen, installing a site blocker with a 10-second countdown, or creating a manual journaling checkpoint before watching content—these are not productivity hacks. They are cognitive rituals. They remind you that what is easy is not always what is right, and that slowing down is sometimes the fastest way to reclaim your time.

What makes friction valuable is not its difficulty but its *directionality*. When thoughtfully placed, it doesn't just obstruct; it orients. It points you back to yourself—not your distracted self, but your choosing self. The one who remembers why they picked up the device in the first place. The one who wants to *live on purpose*, not just respond on autopilot. When friction is treated not as a flaw but as a feature, design becomes less about removing steps, and more about *returning control.*

This is the shift we must embrace—not towards clunkiness, but towards *consciousness by design*. If attention is to be protected, if intention is to lead behaviour, then ease cannot be our only compass. We must learn to value the moment of pause, the point of resistance, the breath before the click. Because often, in that tiny space between desire and action, is where freedom begins.

## Creating Focus Zones

Attention is not abstract. It does not simply happen in the mind. It happens *somewhere*. Every act of focus is also an act of placement—within space, among signals, against distractions. Yet modern digital environments have flattened context so thoroughly that we often forget this. The kitchen becomes the office, the bed becomes the cinema, the phone becomes the therapist, the social feed becomes the public square. When everything happens anywhere, *nothing is anchored*. And when nothing is anchored, attention disperses. We multitask not because we're incapable of focus, but because the environments in which we operate are indifferent to it.

The antidote is not merely willpower. It is *structure*. And not just cognitive or behavioural structure—but spatial structure. Where you do something shapes how you do it. Architects have long understood this. So have monks, composers, chefs, and craftspeople. But digital life has eroded our natural sense of environmental boundary. Focus zones reintroduce that boundary. They are not aesthetic luxuries. They are cognitive technologies.

To create a focus zone is to *declare a purpose for space*. It is to assign a room, a desk, a corner, or a device screen a single, clearly defined cognitive role—work, rest, connection, or creativity—and then defend that role from encroachment. This is more than feng shui. It is behavioural architecture. A home office is not the same thing as a laptop on a bed. A video call taken from the sofa is not the same conversation as one held at a designated table. These things matter because context triggers cues, and cues govern habits. When we fail to define space, space defines us—usually in ways that erode intentionality.

One of the most underappreciated insights from habit science is that environment is the invisible hand of behaviour. In one study, researchers found that people who placed their gym clothes the night before were significantly more likely to exercise the next morning. The reason? *Environmental priming*. The body follows cues. When you design your spaces to signal a specific mode of being—deep work, full rest, genuine conversation—you reduce the friction of entry. You no longer have to "get in the zone" because the zone *gets you*.

This principle is particularly urgent in the age of hybrid work and hyperconnectivity, where physical and digital domains blur. A kitchen table can become a battleground of competing intentions—laptop, phone, food, children, notifications—all coexisting without hierarchy. No wonder focus feels elusive. To counteract this, even minimal spatial cues can help: a separate chair for reading, a specific window view for writing, a physical notebook that is used only during strategy sessions. These cues tell your brain, "Now we're in this mode." They restore boundaries, and with them, mental coherence.

Focus zones are not limited to physical space. They can—and should—extend to the digital layer. A clean desktop, a dedicated browser for work tasks, a minimalist phone home screen—each of these becomes a kind of spatial discipline, a digital room with a declared purpose. Conversely, a cluttered interface is a cognitive smog. If twenty icons scream for your attention the moment you unlock your phone, then the phone is no longer a tool; it's a battleground. Curating digital environments is not pedantry. It is a precondition for agency.

There is also a neurobiological basis for this. The human brain is exquisitely sensitive to context-switching. When you move from composing an email to checking social media, then back to writing, you incur *switching costs*. These costs are not trivial. They degrade working memory, increase mental fatigue, and impair performance. Worse, they fracture narrative continuity—the sense that you are progressing through a thought. Focus zones work because they reduce these switches. They allow the mind to sink into its task without the constant background anxiety of alternative demands.

But designing focus zones is not just about protecting work. It's also about *protecting rest*. In many homes, the bedroom has quietly become a second office. Emails are checked in bed, notifications buzz through the night, and sleep is delayed by the blue-lit scroll. Yet the bedroom is one of the few spaces evolution has wired us to associate with complete surrender. When that association is corrupted, rest becomes fragmented. The solution is not to ban technology, but to *segment its presence*. A charging station in the living room, a no-phone tray by the bed, a rule that devices don't cross a certain threshold—

these are not acts of restriction; they are acts of restoration. They protect the function of the space.

The same applies to zones of *connection*. One of the paradoxes of digital life is that we are constantly communicating but rarely connecting. Screens make it easy to be together but elsewhere. To create a zone of connection is to designate moments and places where attention is undivided. A phone-free dinner table. A ten-minute walk with a partner, uninterrupted by pings. A family couch where TV is communal and phones are exiled. These rituals are not nostalgic. They are neurological. Humans bond through *presence*, and presence requires boundary.

Of course, not everyone has the luxury of a home office, multiple rooms, or even private space. But focus zones are not about square footage. They are about *intention per metre*. A single desk in a shared room can be transformed with small acts of definition: a specific lamp turned on only during deep work, headphones that signal availability status, a small sign that reads "on task." These are cues to self and others. They create islands of focus in the sea of ambient noise.

What is often overlooked is that attention flows where *meaning is located*. If a space feels sacred, we treat it differently. This is why rituals—lighting a candle before writing, closing a laptop with both hands after a work session, taking three breaths before opening a book—are so powerful. They imbue space with significance. They transform rooms into roles. In this sense, a focus zone is not just about what you remove. It's about what you *consecrate*.

Critically, the success of focus zones depends not only on where but on *when*. Temporal zoning—assigning time blocks to specific attentional modes—is just as crucial as spatial zoning. A kitchen table at 8 a.m. can be a workspace; at 6 p.m., a family space. But this shift must be marked. A change in lighting, a new playlist, a closing of tabs—these transitions matter. Without them, boundaries blur and intentions bleed. The result is a kind of attentional static: always on, never fully present.

Focus zones also serve as an antidote to the modern myth that focus is purely personal. The narrative of the willpower hero—someone who resists all temptation through grit alone—is seductive but false. In reality, most high performers *design their environments to make desired behaviours easier and undesired ones harder.* Olympic athletes don't train on the couch. Writers don't compose while scrolling Twitter. They *carve out terrain that supports their cognitive goals.* Focus zones externalise discipline. They make success the default.

Yet it would be reductive to treat focus zones as just tools for productivity. Their deeper function is existential. In a culture that constantly pulls us in multiple directions, to declare a space for single-minded attention is to make a philosophical claim: *I choose depth over drift, presence over noise, intention over reactivity.* That claim is not made once. It is made daily, in the small rituals of spatial design, digital curation, and temporal boundary-setting.

And so the question becomes: where in your life have you allowed environments to dictate attention? Where have signals become so mixed that every space is mediocre at everything? And what would it mean—not just practically, but personally—to reclaim those spaces for clarity?

Focus zones are not a productivity hack. They are an act of self-respect. They say to the world—and more importantly, to yourself—that your attention is worth protecting. That not every moment is open for interruption. That depth is still possible. And that the spaces we shape are, in the end, the ones that shape us.

## From Escape Spaces to Intentional Places

A device is never just a tool. It is an environment, a signal, a ritual, and, increasingly, a space. The screen is where we work, play, scroll, share, avoid, and unwind. In this convergence, something subtle but significant has occurred: the boundary between tool and terrain has collapsed. We no longer simply *use* our phones or laptops; we *enter* them. And once inside, we rarely ask where we are going. In the absence of that question, digital spaces default to one dominant function—*escape.* Not strategic, nourishing, or meaningful escape, but reflexive, numbing withdrawal. The device becomes a portal, not to something chosen, but to whatever algorithm is most profitable in capturing our attention.

This trend is not accidental. Platforms are designed to encourage passive consumption. Their interfaces are engineered for infinite scrolls, autoplay, and algorithmic suggestion loops—all mechanisms that favour time spent over intention held. The cost of this design is rarely discussed in terms of spatial metaphors, but it should be. Because when devices serve primarily as *escape spaces*, they train us to flee discomfort rather than face it, to defer intention rather than declare it. Over time, this erodes both agency and self-definition. When every idle moment becomes an exit, we cease to inhabit the present fully.

To reverse this drift, we must begin treating our devices not as voids to collapse into, but as *places to inhabit deliberately*. This reframing is not poetic—it is pragmatic. Just as a physical room can be designed for rest, focus, conversation, or creation, so too can our digital environments be curated to serve particular cognitive and emotional functions. But to do so, we must begin by confronting the current mismatch between what our devices offer and what our lives require.

Take the smartphone—a device capable of navigation, creativity, communication, learning, and health management. But left uncurated, it becomes a chaos engine: notifications collide, interfaces overwhelm, and one swipe leads to fifteen unintended behaviours. The average user unlocks their phone 58 times a day, often without any clear objective. This is not a failure of discipline. It is a failure of design. *Intention requires architecture.* If everything is accessible everywhere, then nothing feels sacred or significant. This is how devices become spaces of default, not direction.

Redesigning them begins with asking a simple but radical question: *What do I want this device to be for?* Not in general, but *today*. Perhaps your tablet is for deep reading and note-taking. Your phone for light communication and photography. Your laptop for creation, not consumption. Once the function is declared, the environment must be aligned. This means removing apps that conflict with the declared purpose, turning off non-essential notifications, and building home screens around intention, not impulse. It means clearing out digital clutter with the same seriousness as one would prepare a studio or meditation room. Not for aesthetics, but for *psychological orientation.*

One of the most powerful ways to reclaim digital spaces is through the practice of *intentional entry*. This involves not just deciding *what* you will do on a device, but *how you will begin.* Consider the difference between opening a writing app with a clear sentence in mind versus checking email with no specific goal. The former centres purpose. The latter invites drift. By creating rituals around device use—such as taking a breath before unlocking, stating your goal aloud, or entering through a designated app—you activate the prefrontal cortex, interrupting the reflex loop of unconscious engagement. Over time, this practice reconditions your relationship to the device. It becomes a portal to clarity, not confusion.

It is also worth reflecting on the distinction between *escapism* and *restoration.* The former is avoidance dressed as relief; the latter is nourishment that requires awareness. Mindless scrolling in bed may feel like relaxation, but it often leads to disrupted sleep, fragmented thought, and diminished presence. Contrast that with listening to a guided meditation, reading longform journalism, or even watching a well-crafted documentary—all of which are digital activities, but ones that offer return on attention. The difference is not the medium, but the *intention behind the engagement.* Restoration honours your energy. Escapism exploits your inertia.

Digital environments that support restoration must be *deliberately designed.* For example, a phone configured with a "Rest Mode" can limit access to attention-sapping apps, enable blue-light filters, and surface calming music or poetry instead. A laptop "Evening Profile" can dim the screen, close all work-related tabs, and open journaling software. These are not gimmicks. They are architectural decisions. Just as a spa is designed for relaxation and a classroom for learning, a device can be made to signal restoration or inquiry—if we bother to design it that way.

There is also a broader cultural issue at play. Our society tends to dichotomise technology as either saviour or saboteur. But this binary is lazy. It relieves us of responsibility by outsourcing agency to the object itself. In reality, technology is neither neutral nor deterministic. It is *responsive.* It reflects and amplifies the values of its user—or its designer. If we want our devices to become intentional places, we must adopt the mindset of *custodianship.* This means taking responsibility for how these tools are configured, when they are accessed, and what they are allowed to influence.

Consider how musicians treat their instruments. A violinist does not leave their bow tangled in laundry. A pianist does not balance coffee cups on their keyboard. Their tools are sacred. Their configurations matter. The same reverence can—and should—be applied to digital tools. Not because they are inherently worthy of it, but because *we are.* Our attention, cognition, and creativity deserve environments that support—not scatter—them.

The shift from escape spaces to intentional places also invites a reevaluation of what digital time is *for.* Is it for learning? For building? For connecting with loved ones? For aligning with long-term goals? Each of these functions can be supported by digital tools—if the tools are intentionally structured. But when these purposes are not made explicit, devices revert to serving only the lowest common denominator of stimulation. They entertain but do not enrich. They consume time without honouring it.

This reframing requires effort. It is far easier to accept the default interface, scroll what is offered, and blame the tool when attention fails. But intentionality is a muscle. It strengthens through use. Start with one interface. Ask: *What do I want this space to feel like?* Then ask: *What does it currently do to my mind?* That gap is your design brief.

Critically, this shift is not about abstinence. It is about *alignment.* The goal is not to remove devices from life, but to remove randomness from device use. Just as you would not walk into a restaurant and eat whatever is put in front of you without inquiry, you should not enter digital space without conscious selection. The stakes are too high. Time, focus, energy, and values are all on the line.

Devices can be theatres of distraction or theatres of depth. They can be casinos or classrooms. Libraries or echo chambers. The difference lies not in the code, but in the *construction of the user's intention.* You can choose what you want your phone to stand for, what your browser opens to, what your notifications declare about your priorities. Every configuration is a vote—for your future self or against it.

From escape spaces to intentional places: this is the architecture of modern attention. It is not built in silicon or glass, but in habits, cues, rituals, and declarations. It begins the moment you unlock your device and ask, *Why am I here?* If that question becomes your compass, every digital interaction becomes a design opportunity. Not to flee, but to arrive. Not to escape, but to engage. Not to lose yourself, but to find clarity within the very tools that once scattered you.

# Chapter 9
# When Tech Serves You

Technology becomes perilous not through sheer frequency of use, but through thoughtlessness. The danger lies not in hours logged online, but in the absence of discernment behind them. Ubiquity is often mistaken for necessity, utility for alignment, and connectivity for nourishment. Rarely do we pause to ask: is this tool serving me—or have I begun serving it? This chapter pivots from reactive avoidance to deliberate integration. Not all technology undermines attention; in fact, when chosen intentionally, some tools can act as scaffolds for clarity, focus, and agency. The challenge is not abstinence, but mastery.

Most people inherit their digital lives rather than design them. Apps accumulate reactively, default settings remain, notifications pile up like cluttered hallways, and routines crystallise not from strategy, but from repetition. The cognitive architecture of daily life becomes quietly shaped by external incentives. Without explicit consent, we are tethered to platforms that nudge behaviour with silent imperatives: "respond," "scroll," "refresh," "post." Each act is trivial in isolation, yet collectively they fragment attention and dilute intentionality.

The hidden cost of indiscriminate tech use is subtle but profound. Focus splinters. Priorities blur. Time leaks unnoticed. One is constantly active yet rarely progressing. The solution is not retreat, asceticism, or moralistic warnings about "screen time." It is disciplined curation—posing questions artists, philosophers, and strategists have long asked: what do I want to create? What life do I intend to lead? Which tools genuinely support that vision?

Reclaiming technological agency requires more than deletion; it requires alignment. Digital tools are not created equal. Some monetise distraction; others fortify intention. Recognising the difference is a cognitive and moral imperative. A thoughtfully organised calendar, a note-taking system that sharpens thought, a mindfulness tracker that reinforces self-awareness—these are not indulgences, but architects of mental clarity. Used wisely, the right tool does not constrain autonomy; it amplifies it.

Frameworks, not lists of apps, guide this process. Enter Digital Sabbaths and Usage Cycles. Regenerative systems thrive on rhythm: crops rotate, athletes recover, writers alternate incubation and output. The mind is no different. Constant, unmodulated digital access deprives it of rest, novelty, and synthesis. Regular breaks—daily, weekly, seasonal—serve as renewal rather than punishment. They recalibrate the mind without disengaging from life entirely.

Take the Sunday Digital Sabbath as a practical example. Professionals adopt a 24-hour window without optional screens—not as a lifestyle manifesto, but as intentional pause. Deep reading, walking without headphones, unstructured reflection, slow conversation—these moments cultivate perspective rather than detachment. Over time, such rituals allow technology to serve, rather than dominate, cognition.

This perspective becomes the lens through which alignment is assessed. Use alone does not equal usefulness. Popularity, frictionless design, or apparent productivity does not guarantee compatibility with values. Mapping habits against goals demands reflection: what does this platform do to my thinking, energy, and relationships—and does that serve my priorities? Networking apps can feel performative rather than connective; educational platforms can encourage shallow engagement. Misalignment is rarely the user's fault; it signals design at odds with intention.

Reclaiming alignment means charting one's attention landscape. Which apps merit a place on the home screen, and why? Which platforms claim mornings, and which none at all? Which tools reflect ambitions, and which divert them? Honest answers require criteria and discernment—knowing when to adapt, when to quit.

Quitting is not failure; sometimes it is insight. Some platforms cannot be reshaped to serve deeper goals, no matter the adjustments. Others can be integrated with boundaries or time limits. The distinction matters: adaptation for the malleable, deletion for the fundamentally misaligned.

This process demands moral clarity and tolerance for social friction. Saying no to widely used platforms can provoke FOMO or feelings of irrelevance. Yet selective abstention often yields a deeper inclusion—not in every conversation, but in the right ones. Clarity emerges not from minimalism, but from confidence in choices that reflect values.

When technology serves its user, coherence follows. Devices echo priorities. Tools support thought. Rhythms mirror needs. This coherence is deliberate, not accidental. It does not demand perfection, only conscious design: auditing relationships with tools, choosing sabbaths, declaring non-negotiables, refusing to render attention an open-access resource.

The most effective technology is intentional. It functions as mirror, collaborator, and scaffold—present when needed, absent when focus matters most. This chapter is not about software installation; it is about installing sovereignty. Life is finite. The mind is precious. Time deserves tools that know the difference.

## Smart Tools for Mindful Use

The most dangerous myth about technology is that its impact is determined solely by how much time we spend with it. In reality, *it's how deliberately we engage with it*—what tools we choose, how we configure them, and what underlying psychological patterns they support—that shapes whether it sharpens our attention or scatters it. The same screen can be either a portal to deep focus or a trapdoor into digital entropy. Tools, like environments, are never neutral. They are embedded with assumptions, incentives, and defaults that cue certain behaviours. The question for the thoughtful user is not whether to use technology, but *how to audit and choose tools that reinforce clarity, intentionality, and attention* rather than dilute them.

Modern digital infrastructure is designed for ubiquity, not discernment. Notifications are enabled by default, attention is constantly solicited, and multitasking is normalised. It takes considerable intentionality to opt out of the noise and configure a cognitive ecosystem that supports reflective rather than reactive thinking. Yet such a design is possible. There is a growing ecosystem of tools—some analogue in spirit, some digitally native—that do not merely promise productivity but actually *cultivate presence.* These are not magic solutions. They don't automate wisdom or discipline. But they do *reduce friction for better decisions*, act as scaffolds for focus, and remind us of values we might otherwise forget in the flux of modern attention demands.

Take the example of note-taking. A platform like Notion offers infinite flexibility, but that very flexibility can encourage over-structuring and surface-level engagement. In contrast, a tool like Obsidian, which is local-first, markdown-based, and intentionally minimalist, encourages slower, more deliberate thought. It doesn't nudge users to publish or share or turn notes into clickbait. It rewards *thinking in layers*, linking thoughts rather than broadcasting them. The tool's design constraints subtly cue reflection over reaction. Likewise, for those who prefer analogue methods, the simple act of writing with pen and paper—say, in a Muji notebook or Leuchtturm journal—can restore a tactile relationship with thought. The slowness is not a drawback. It is the *feature* that fosters depth.

In the realm of time management, there is a subtle but important distinction between tools that encourage *compression* versus those that foster *clarity.* Many task managers reward busyness: long lists, badges, deadlines, and integrations that make it easy to stack more into your day than it can reasonably hold. In contrast, a tool like Timeular—which visualises time via a physical tracker—or analogue time-blocking methods like the Full Focus Planner, promote *constraint.* They require the user to *choose fewer, better things*, and to live with those choices rather than endlessly shuffle priorities. These tools don't merely track tasks—they shape mindset. They reinforce the philosophy that *clarity precedes efficiency*, and that not everything that can be done should be.

The same principle holds for browser environments. Mainstream browsers are loaded with distractions by default—bookmarks bars, frequent site visits, and cookies that follow you from one dopamine-loop to another. But it is entirely possible to redesign your digital gateway. Tools like Arc and Brave provide ways to strip the interface down to its essentials. Paired with extensions like Momentum (a minimalist homepage with a single daily intention) or Workona (which organises tabs by context and project), the browsing experience can become a conscious, intentional act rather than a passive fall into habitual checking. These tools don't prevent distraction, but they *nudge toward discernment*, much like clearing a cluttered desk before beginning serious work.

More directly, tools like Freedom, Cold Turkey, and One Sec operate not at the level of content but at the level of access and interruption. Freedom lets users block entire categories of sites across devices during focus sessions. Cold Turkey can lock down your entire system if needed. One Sec takes a subtler approach: it inserts a mandatory breath and reflection prompt before launching habit-forming apps. What these tools share is not authoritarian restriction, but *deliberate friction*. They help the user *remember* their intentions at the very moment they're most likely to act out of impulse. This isn't digital asceticism. It's *environmental design for better impulse control*—a design that externalises the internal principle of mindfulness.

But mindfulness tools themselves have become a paradoxical category. Meditation apps often replicate the very dynamics they claim to counter: streaks, badges, push reminders, and an ever-expanding library of content that invites the same shallow grazing as social media. The most effective tools in this space tend to focus not on consumption, but *presence-building*. Consider Insight Timer's timer function without any guided content, or the minimalist interface of Oak. These are not platforms designed to become habit loops. They are *aids to silence*, not replacements for it. Similarly, the growing use of ambient sound platforms like Endel—designed to align with circadian rhythms and cognitive states—offers a sonic environment that doesn't demand attention but *supports* it. They don't compete with the mind—they cushion it.

There is also a category of tools that support *meta-awareness*. Tools like RescueTime or Screen Time on iOS don't just track usage—they reveal patterns. But the key lies in *how* those patterns are interpreted. If they become sources of guilt, they simply replicate the self-surveillance of productivity culture. But if used as mirrors—quiet, non-judgemental reflections of where energy is going—they can be powerful prompts for reflection. Similarly, journaling tools like Day One (digital) or The Five Minute Journal (analogue) create space to externalise thoughts, review attention, and reset intentions. What matters most is *not the tracking itself*, but *how the data is framed*—not as performance metrics, but as *aids to self-inquiry*.

One of the most underappreciated tools for mindful tech use is the *home screen*. Not as a passive interface, but as a designed space. Moving high-friction apps off the first page, or even removing them entirely, changes the default launch patterns. Replacing them with shortcuts to a journal, a reading list, or a values document reframes your phone from a stimulus machine to a *portal to intention*. This may sound like a cosmetic tweak. It's not. It's an *architectural change*. Just as open-plan offices affect how people speak and think, *interface placement shapes behaviour*. When the first thing you see cues a mindful state, it sets a tone that cascades into how you relate to the device as a whole.

Still, it is important to acknowledge that no tool is a panacea. A mindful person can use any technology well, while a scattered mind will find distraction even in a blank text file. *Tools reveal, they do not replace, the inner posture of the user.* This is why the process of tool selection must begin with clarity of intent. What are you optimising for—output or presence? What does focus mean in your specific context? What are you willing to sacrifice for it? Once those questions are answered, tools can become true allies—not because they eliminate complexity, but because they *honour your complexity with structure*.

Ultimately, the best tools do not shout. They do not add noise. They *support stillness*. They are frictionless only in service of intentionality, and difficult only in ways that discourage impulse. They respect your autonomy. They assume you are capable of directing your own attention, but sometimes need scaffolding to do so. And they never pretend to be the end goal. The point is never the app. The point is *what kind of mind you are trying to inhabit*, and what kind of life you are trying to live through it.

To live deliberately in a distracted world requires more than willpower. It requires *infrastructure*. Not infrastructure imposed by algorithms, but *infrastructure crafted through discernment.* Smart tools, wisely chosen, help create that scaffolding—not because they make us better, but because they remind us of who we already intended to be.

## Digital Sabbaths and Usage Cycles

If a technology requires your constant presence to deliver value, it owns you. Periods of disconnection are not simply optional luxuries; they are diagnostic tests. The ability—or inability—to step away from a digital environment and return refreshed is not merely a matter of personal discipline; it is a metric of whether that system supports human flourishing or erodes it. Just as muscle requires rest to rebuild stronger, cognition and attention depend on rhythm. Without structured intervals of pause, even the most enriching digital environments begin to calcify into habit loops, and attention atrophies into passive scrolling. The concept of a *Digital Sabbath*—a recurring, intentional period of disconnection—is neither nostalgic nor Luddite. It is an act of system-level self-respect. It restores perspective not because it offers escape, but because it interrupts habituation. And the rhythm of *usage cycles*—how often, when, and why we engage—matters as much as the tools we use.

There's a reason almost every major spiritual tradition includes sabbath, silence, or fasting. The human mind is not designed for uninterrupted intake. It requires contrast to discern signal from noise, space to metabolise experience into insight. In the digital realm, however, the frictionless nature of access eliminates all natural boundaries. There is no physical distance between the self and the source of stimulation. No sunset or sabbath bell that reminds us to stop. And so, one swipe bleeds into the next, not because we are weak-willed but because *the environment lacks markers of completion.* Sabbath, in its modern digital form, is not about withdrawal but about *renegotiating boundaries*. It says: "This is when I *am not available* to systems that profit from my availability."

The practice is deceptively simple: a full day without screens, typically once per week. But the implications are profound. First, it requires confronting how many small frictions and fears surface when access is cut. What if I miss something? What if someone needs me? What if I feel bored? These are not technical questions—they are existential ones. They force a reckoning with *what presence has been outsourced to the feed.* Digital sabbaths restore the right to reinhabit one's own nervous system, to allow thought to unfurl at its natural tempo, to let a moment last longer than the dopamine half-life of a notification.

The most successful Sabbath practices are ritualised but not rigid. They honour the intent of interruption without moralising the method. Some choose Friday sundown to Saturday sundown. Others begin their Sabbath at whatever point they feel most worn. The key is *repeatability*, not perfection. Recurring breaks work not because they are dramatic but because they are rhythmic. They allow *mental reset points* to be scheduled, anticipated, and internalised—like knowing that a room will be cleaned weekly, or that an inbox will not be opened on Sundays. Even if chaos erupts during the week, that anchor point remains. And this predictability creates a psychological perimeter within which *real recovery* can occur.

But digital sabbaths are only one axis of the broader architecture of usage cycles. The goal is not just rest, but *intelligent patterning.* Attention is not a faucet—it is a tide. Knowing when to be fully online, when to taper, and when to disconnect entirely allows us to align our digital presence with our physiological and emotional capacity. Tools like Timeboxing (allocating specific windows for email or social media), Seasonal Resets (where users delete or suspend accounts during particular months), or Platform Rotation (cycling through apps for different quarters of the year) create *adaptive rhythms.* These do not reject technology. They *place it within the cadence of a larger life*, where it supports rather than defines the day.

Take the example of Cal Newport's "Digital Minimalism" approach, which encourages a 30-day digital detox followed by reintroduction based on strict criteria of value. While some critique it as extreme, it highlights an essential truth: *absence is clarifying.* We cannot assess a tool's actual utility while under its influence. Stepping away creates contrast. We learn what we miss, and what we merely reached for out of reflex. Likewise, platforms like Instagram or LinkedIn may offer great professional value *only in seasonal bursts.* A photographer might use Instagram for portfolio building during launch season, then archive the app for two months of creative gestation. A jobseeker may benefit from LinkedIn's network density during a search, but find that its ambient anxiety is corrosive once the job is secured. These are not contradictions—they are *contextual calibrations*. And cycles allow for this nuance to emerge.

Of course, any discussion of cycles must also contend with the false binary between online and offline. It's not just *when* we disconnect—it's *how* we return. A sabbath that leads to Monday morning inbox triage, flooded with algorithmic catch-up prompts, is not a net gain. That's why *re-entry design* matters. Some practitioners of digital rest include buffer rituals at the end of a break: a journal entry to reflect on insights, a physical list of what to reintroduce, or even a short walk before opening the first app. These practices signal to the nervous system that re-entry is conscious, not compulsive. They *honour the boundary just crossed*, and reduce the velocity of the return.

Critics of digital sabbaths sometimes argue that disconnection is a privilege—one only available to those whose livelihoods or communities are not tied to real-time responsiveness. There's validity here. For many, being reachable is a requirement. But even in high-responsibility environments, *partial sabbaths* can work. For example, one might keep the phone on for emergencies but uninstall high-friction apps. Or restrict input to SMS and calls only. Or automate "unavailable" auto-replies during sabbath hours. The point is not purism. It's *deliberate reduction*, calibrated to each person's constraints. What matters is not a rigid definition of "off," but the cultivation of *periods without algorithmic intrusion*.

Importantly, sabbaths are not about self-denial. They are about *reclaiming default*. They say: "For this period, I will not optimise, publish, consume, or compete. I will simply be." In doing so, they create *psychological spaciousness* that modern interface design works hard to eliminate. For many, the first few sabbaths are uncomfortable. This is to be expected. In the absence of constant inputs, the self is louder. Thought is unfiltered. But this is where *integration happens*. Sabbaths teach us not to fear stillness. And through that stillness, a different quality of attention emerges—less reactive, more grounded, less enamoured with novelty, more attuned to depth.

There is a reason some of the most enduring intellectual traditions were built on cycles. Academic calendars alternate between terms and breaks. Monastic routines include vigils and matins. Even the act of breathing includes exhale, pause, and inhale. Usage cycles are not an invention—they are a *reclamation* of this ancient cadence. And when we apply them to the digital realm, we are not imposing artificial rules—we are *restoring biological rhythm to environments that have overridden it.*

This is not romanticism. It is strategy. A knowledge worker who begins the week with a Sunday sabbath is not behind—they are *ahead*, mentally clear and less burdened by the scatter of unchecked inputs. A family that sets Saturday device-free hours is not disconnected—they are *more connected*, relationally and emotionally. A student who uninstalls Reddit during exam season is not out of touch—they are *fully present* to the work of learning. These are not sacrifices. They are acts of *alignment.* They ensure that the rhythm of digital life does not drown out the deeper pulse of human life.

Ultimately, usage cycles and digital sabbaths are about *redistribution of power.* They reassign the authority to set tempo away from the platform and back to the individual. They remind us that engagement is a choice, and that saying "no" is not a protest—it is *a pattern interrupt*, a pause that makes intention possible again. When designed with clarity, these cycles don't just improve wellbeing. They preserve sovereignty. They turn time from a resource spent to *a rhythm reclaimed.*

## Aligning Use with Values

If a tool shapes your attention more than you shape its purpose, it is no longer serving you. The difference between mindful technology use and unconscious compulsion often lies in a simple but underexplored distinction: alignment. Not between tool and task, but between *tool and self.* A device is not inherently beneficial because it's efficient, nor is an app worthwhile simply because it saves time. The core question—rarely asked, even among high-functioning users—is: *Does this technology serve the life I'm trying to live?* Without a values-based reference point, even the most disciplined tech habits become unmoored, drifting toward convenience rather than congruence. The aim is not digital abstinence, but *deliberate integration.* To use technology as a means of expressing values—not just achieving outcomes.

Modern digital culture is rife with optimisation—track more, automate more, consume faster. Yet efficiency without intentionality is a form of drift. You may achieve more while becoming less of who you meant to be. This misalignment is rarely dramatic; it accrues subtly. A writer uses their phone's note app for creativity but finds that their instinct to open it is now tied to checking email. A parent downloads educational videos for their child but notices that the app's autoplay algorithm ends in content antithetical to the values they meant to nurture. A student joins a networking platform for career growth and ends up measuring their worth in likes and follower counts. These are not failures of the user—they are *failures of alignment.* When values are not explicitly linked to usage, the environment defines the goal.

To realign, one must first articulate what matters. This isn't a moral exercise—it's a strategic one. Values function as a compass, not a code of conduct. They allow us to evaluate not only what we're doing but *why* and *how* we're doing it. A professional who values deep work will structure their digital life differently than someone who prizes community responsiveness. The first might disable all push notifications, use website blockers, and maintain device-free hours to safeguard flow. The second may curate messaging tools, schedule regular digital check-ins, and intentionally use social media to amplify causes. Both may spend equal time online, but the *shape of their engagement* reflects their priorities.

This principle becomes especially powerful when applied to platform relationships. A key question: *What is the platform optimising for, and is that the same thing I care about?* Instagram optimises for attention. Twitter (or its successors) amplify conflict and immediacy. YouTube chases watch time. None of these objectives are inherently malicious, but they are often *orthogonal* to user wellbeing. If you value clarity, compassion, or sustained learning, your relationship with these platforms must be *actively mediated.* That might mean changing default settings, disabling autoplay, unfollowing high-noise accounts, or deliberately repurposing a platform. For example, some users convert Instagram into a visual journaling tool—uploading only what they want to remember, following no one. Others use Twitter solely as a writing discipline—posting ideas but not reading replies. These are not tricks—they are acts of *functional re-ownership.*

Importantly, alignment does not mean every tool must match every value. Life is pluralistic. But there should be no ongoing contradiction between how you use technology and what you claim to care about. If your calendar is filled with Zoom calls and Slack pings but you say you value presence, there is a misalignment that deserves scrutiny. If your screen time is dominated by news and productivity hacks but your stated goal is spiritual growth or emotional regulation, the question is not whether the apps are good or bad—it's *whether they fit.* This doesn't mean abandoning everything that doesn't serve your highest value. It means *being able to name the trade-off and accept it consciously.*

There's also a developmental arc to value-tech alignment. What works during one life stage may not serve another. Early-career professionals often value access and visibility; later, they may crave focus and boundaries. New parents shift from curiosity-driven browsing to stability-oriented routines. Burnout survivors may move from hyper-availability to radical containment. Each shift in values requires a recalibration of the tech environment. And this re-alignment is not one-and-done. It is cyclical, seasonal, and contextual. That's why it's helpful to revisit usage periodically—not just to see *what's working*, but to ask *who am I becoming through these habits?*

One powerful exercise involves creating a "tech values map." Begin with a list of your top five personal or professional values. Then, list your top ten digital tools or platforms. Draw lines between each tool and the values it supports—or undermines. For each connection, articulate *how* it supports that value: through enabling, expressing, protecting, or amplifying it. If no line can be drawn, that's a red flag. If a tool supports a value in one domain but contradicts another, consider if it can be constrained to context. For instance, Reddit might support curiosity but erode calm. Can it be time-boxed to Sunday mornings only? Can its content be filtered? Can the platform be swapped for a more aligned alternative, like a longform publication or research database?

Alignment is also about recognising *how values show up*—not just what they are. Two people may both value knowledge, but one expresses it through solitary study, the other through collaborative debate. Their digital ecosystems should reflect that nuance. It's not enough to say "I use this to learn." The better question is: *What kind of learning does this tool enable, and is that the kind I seek?* The same applies to values like connection, creativity, or freedom. For some, connection means voice notes and longform writing; for others, it's group chats or forums. For some, freedom means reducing external inputs; for others, it's the capacity to explore. When tech is selected and configured to honour these subtleties, usage becomes a form of integrity.

To be clear, perfect alignment is aspirational, not achievable in all contexts. The modern work environment often mandates tools that conflict with our personal rhythms. Many people are required to use platforms that are noisy, surveillance-prone, or ethically dubious. In these cases, *boundary layering* becomes essential. That might mean restricting access to work tools to certain hours, separating work and personal devices, or creating rituals that "seal off" the psychological residue of those tools after use. Even within systems we can't control, we can exert agency over *how we relate* to them.

Equally important is the idea that alignment requires *experiential honesty*. It's one thing to intend for a tool to serve a value; it's another to track whether it actually does. You may download a meditation app to support inner peace but find that its gamified streaks make you anxious. You might install a reading app to learn more deeply but find that its UX keeps pulling you toward summaries and quotes rather than immersive engagement. In these moments, values serve not as a guilt-inducing yardstick but a feedback loop. They allow us to revise not from shame, but from clarity. A values-aligned digital life is not perfect. It is *transparent*, *iterative*, and *anchored in what matters*.

This alignment has ripple effects. When tech use reflects personal values, *motivation becomes intrinsic*. You no longer need to guilt yourself into reduced screen time or forced focus. Instead, you engage—or disengage—with tools from a place of coherence. Your identity is not threatened by disconnection because the connection itself is *an extension of who you are*, not a performance or obligation. This reduces the cognitive dissonance that drives burnout and makes self-regulation feel burdensome. In other words, alignment makes discipline feel like a form of dignity—not deprivation.

Finally, aligning tech use with values reinforces *psychological sovereignty*. When your environment reflects your priorities, you are no longer navigating with borrowed metrics. You measure success not in click-throughs, streaks, or followers but in resonance, presence, and integrity. You exit the loop of comparison and return to the grounded work of becoming. And in a culture that profits from your distraction, this is no small act. It is, in many ways, the quietest and most radical form of resistance: to live a life that reflects your values—not your feed.

## When to Quit, When to Adapt

There's a moment—usually quiet, often private—when a tool that once energised begins to feel extractive. The platform that promised connection now saps energy. The app you once used to learn now loops you into mindless repetition. This shift is subtle but telling. What began as empowerment has turned into obligation, or worse, erosion. And yet, we hesitate to leave. Part of the complexity of modern digital life lies in this dilemma: the question is rarely "Is this bad?" but "Is this still *good enough* to keep?" Inertia, FOMO, and sunk costs conspire to keep us tethered to digital environments that no longer align with our goals—or our integrity. Knowing *when to quit and when to adapt* is not just a matter of productivity. It is a matter of sovereignty.

Modern platforms are not passive tools; they are dynamic ecosystems, calibrated to evolve in ways that serve the company first and the user second. What you signed up for in 2016 may bear little resemblance to the current feature set or content norms. A writing tool may now function more like a publishing platform. A chat app may have been optimised for group collaboration but has pivoted toward team surveillance. A social network once centred on mutual discovery may now amplify celebrity, controversy, and performative identity. These shifts are rarely announced. They're felt as friction: a decrease in fulfilment, a spike in reactivity, a creeping sense of dissonance. And still, many users continue, trapped by habit or the fear of missing out.

To decide whether to quit or adapt, one must begin with *honest appraisal*, not habitual loyalty. The first question is not "Do I still use it?" but "Do I still *want* to use it?" And if so, "Under what conditions does this tool still serve me?" This is where many people conflate discomfort with dysfunction. Not all friction is bad. But when discomfort stems from *misalignment*, from the tool shaping you in ways you didn't consent to, it's a signal. Continuing in spite of that signal is not resilience—it is neglect.

A clear-eyed cost-benefit analysis can help disentangle this. Ask: What value does this platform provide me, *today*? Not what it promised. Not what others extract from it. What *I* get, and what I trade for it. Then list the cognitive, emotional, and temporal costs: how often do I check it reflexively? What emotions dominate after use? Do I leave it feeling clearer or more fragmented? Am I drawn in by purpose or compulsion? This kind of audit often reveals that usage persists not because of net benefit, but because the platform has become *ambient*: a default behaviour rather than a deliberate choice.

Sometimes, adaptation—not deletion—is the wiser path. The same platform that fragments your attention might be redeemed through constraint. Twitter, for instance, may be a toxic timesink if consumed unfiltered, yet become a generative space when used only for outbound writing, or via a curated list of thinkers. LinkedIn might induce status anxiety when scrolled aimlessly, but function well as a monthly publishing channel if stripped of notifications and limited to a posting calendar. Instagram, so often dismissed as a vanity feed, can be repurposed into a private visual log, a moodboard, or an accountability diary. The key lies not in rejecting the tool wholesale, but in *refining its function to reflect your purpose.*

However, some platforms are resistant to reconfiguration. This is especially true when *the platform's business model* depends on friction, addiction, or user manipulation. You can't meaningfully adapt a tool designed to override your attention. You can't force intentional use from a system optimised for endless engagement. In these cases, the question becomes not how to adjust, but how to *exit.* And here, timing is critical. Too early, and you may miss potential growth. Too late, and you've sacrificed months—or years—of attention to a platform that no longer supports your evolution.

One meaningful indicator for quitting is *pattern recognition*. If you've reconfigured a platform multiple times, set boundaries, reinstalled it with new rules, and still find yourself regretting its influence, that's not a failure of discipline. It's a design feature. Platforms that undermine your goals even after deliberate adaptation aren't broken—they're functioning *as intended*, just not in your favour. Quitting then becomes an act of discernment, not defeat. You're not escaping responsibility. You're reasserting it.

There's also a psychological liberation that comes from strategic quitting. Deleting a platform that no longer aligns doesn't just free up time—it clears mental residue. The energy previously spent managing impulses, guilt, or self-rationalisation can be redirected to more coherent efforts. Moreover, quitting allows space for *alternatives* to emerge. Many users find that once they delete a distracting platform, they rediscover dormant habits—reading deeply, reaching out to friends directly, writing, or simply resting without a screen. These gains are not "replacements" in the digital sense—they are *reclaims* in the human one.

Still, quitting is rarely straightforward. For some, platforms are entangled with identity, income, or community. An artist might depend on Instagram to reach clients. A writer may build their readership on Substack. A remote worker might rely on Slack or Discord for professional relevance. In such cases, the question isn't "Can I quit?" but "Can I *compartmentalise*?" Can I separate the role-based necessity of the platform from my personal life? Can I firewall the platform's influence to professional hours only? Can I create rituals to enter and exit that digital space with intention? These micro-borders can be powerful safeguards against unintentional enmeshment.

What's often missing in digital hygiene conversations is *permission to outgrow a platform*. The internet is filled with productivity advice that treats platforms as immutable—tools to be mastered, rather than environments to be evaluated. But growth often means *graduating* from certain digital spaces. A platform that served you in one life season may not serve you now. Letting go isn't failure—it's evolution. And the more self-aware your digital life becomes, the more often you'll face this decision point: *Adapt or exit?* Neither path is right by default. But indecision is itself a decision—with consequences.

Ultimately, there is no universal formula for when to quit or when to adapt. But there *is* a universal responsibility: to remain the author of your attention. Every platform you use shapes your thinking, habits, and identity. That shaping must never be passive. Whether you stay or go, reframe or release, the core practice is the same: *conscious sovereignty*. Not just managing tools, but curating the psychological environments in which your values live—or erode. In this sense, quitting is not a break from discipline. It is its most refined expression: knowing what to walk away from, and having the courage to do so without apology.

# Chapter 10
# Raising Screenwise Kids

If we wish to grasp the impact of digital life on children, the clearest lens is often the adults around them. The average parent spends more time gazing at screens than meeting their child's eyes. This is not a critique; it is a reflection. For today's young people, the family serves as the first interface, the home as the first platform, and parents as the earliest algorithm to be anticipated. In such an environment, digital literacy is not something taught through instruction—it is absorbed through example.

Parenting in this era is less about filters, timers, or bans than about modelling discernment. A child's sense of boundaries, attention, and self-worth is shaped more by what parents do than what they say. When a parent scrolls through messages during dinner while cautioning about "too much screen time," the lesson is in the contradiction. Young children, especially, learn through imitation, which is guided by exposure rather than intent.

The task, therefore, is not merely to raise "screen-literate" children, but screenwise ones—able to navigate the digital world without being consumed by it. Achieving this requires more than cautionary tales about the internet or visions of a tech-free upbringing. It calls for a nuanced understanding that blends developmental psychology, cognitive science, digital ethics, and family dynamics. In short, it demands adults willing to examine their own habits before instructing their children.

Consider the developmental reality: children's executive functions—the neurological systems that regulate focus, decision-making, and self-control—remain under construction well into adolescence. Screens, with their rapid cycles of novelty and feedback, can short-circuit these systems if exposure is excessive or unmoderated. Not all screen time is harmful; context, content, and co-engagement matter. A child watching a thoughtfully paced educational programme with a parent experiences an entirely different effect than one hopping from TikTok clip to clip in isolation. The former encourages co-regulation and learning; the latter erodes attention and internal calm.

Yet too often, discourse around screens reduces to binaries: good versus bad, tech-savvy versus tech-free, supervision versus independence. Such framings fail to reflect reality: screens are omnipresent, structuring schooling, socialisation, entertainment, and logistics. Denial is naïve; unexamined acceptance is negligent. The challenge is integration: equipping children to engage deliberately, with agency and awareness.

This begins by recognising that parental control alone is insufficient. Control without coherence is performative. Reliance on apps or external enforcement without modelling internal discipline leads children to internalise inconsistency. They become adept at managing appearances—adhering to rules when observed, circumventing them when not. What they miss is the deeper rationale: why disengage, why pause, why prioritise presence over passive absorption. Motivation of this depth must be cultivated, not imposed.

Collaborative tech agreements provide one path forward. Families can establish shared principles and rhythms—rituals that signal moments for connection, reflection, or rest. These are not enforceable contracts but cultural tools, calibrated to values and developmental stage. A five-year-old may need structured routines with visual timers and screen-free zones; a teenager may benefit from co-created agreements rooted in mutual reasoning. In both cases, the goal is internalised judgment—skills that persist into adulthood, beyond parental oversight.

Understanding brain development is crucial. Frequent early screen use correlates with changes in white matter integrity, affecting language, attention, and executive function. Rapid-reward media may reduce tolerance for tasks requiring sustained focus: reading long texts, solving complex problems, engaging in unstructured play. Screens are not inherently harmful; they shape cognitive defaults.

Teaching attention is central—not as coercion but as practice. The capacity to wait, observe, or daydream is increasingly endangered.

Parents can protect and nurture it by structuring open time, providing analogue tools, and creating low-interruption zones. Simple choices—keeping devices out of bedrooms, prioritising phone-free meals, modelling routines of device absence—accumulate over time. These measures are not restrictions; they are scaffolding for developing minds.

Boredom, too, must be reappraised. In digital culture, it is often viewed as failure. Developmentally, it is a crucible. Children left to encounter boredom learn to generate, rather than consume: writing, building, inventing. These acts cultivate imagination, initiative, and resilience—but they require parents willing to tolerate discomfort without immediate screen-based intervention. "I trust you to figure this out" is not neglect; it is a vote of confidence in their creative faculties.

Equally, parents must interrogate their own screen use. Devices offer relief, distraction, and brief reprieves. But when children observe adults using screens to manage stress or boredom, they internalise those strategies. Presence appears optional; immediacy trumps patience; screens replace engagement. Rewriting these patterns demands honesty and grace rather than guilt.

The aim is not to cultivate miniature monks renouncing all digital tools, nor hyper-regulated perfectionists. It is to raise children capable of discerning their digital relationships, understanding what energises them and what depletes, and acting with awareness. This capacity emerges not from strict control or unbounded freedom, but from consistent modelling, open dialogue, and reflective practice.

The stakes extend beyond childhood. Habits formed now will shape relationships, work, rest, and selfhood for decades. Children inherit a digital grammar unless guided to question it. Parents, imperfect though they may be, play the pivotal role: prioritising presence over performance, wisdom over optimisation, connection over mere compliance. Raising screenwise children begins not with limiting devices, but with reclaiming one's own attention and offering it fully to them.

## Children Imitate More Than They Obey

A child's education begins not with the spoken word but with the silent gesture. Long before they can articulate a coherent sentence or interpret a household rule, children observe. They are exquisitely attuned not to what adults say, but to what adults do. This is not a quirk of childhood—it is a feature. Evolution has equipped young minds to absorb the patterns, rituals, and emotional cues embedded in their environment, especially those exhibited by the most influential figures in their lives: their caregivers. When it comes to technology use, the implications of this are profound. We can remind children to "put down the iPad" or insist they "go outside and play," but if those commands are issued while we ourselves are staring into a glowing screen, the message is not only muted—it is contradicted.

Modelling has always been more powerful than instruction, but in the digital age, this principle has gained both urgency and complexity. The device in a parent's hand is no longer just a communication tool; it is an entire ecosystem of stimuli—emails, news, alerts, dopamine loops—that children can sense even if they don't yet understand. A distracted gaze, a half-present nod, or a habitual phone check at the dinner table does more to sculpt a child's digital instincts than any lecture on screen time limits. This is not simply about hypocrisy; it's about neurological development. Mirror neurons—those cellular mechanisms that fire both when an action is performed and when it is observed—are hard at work during these moments. Children are not learning about boundaries from our rules; they are internalising our defaults.

Consider a typical household in which a parent tells their child, "Only one hour of games today," then proceeds to spend the rest of the evening toggling between work emails and social media feeds. To the child, the rule feels arbitrary and the adult world hypocritical. Over time, this can seed not only resentment but also a distorted hierarchy of tech use: devices are for grown-ups to indulge in, and for children to be rationed. In fact, studies in developmental psychology increasingly suggest that perceived inconsistency between what parents preach and what they practice erodes a child's internal regulation. Far from learning discipline, they learn that the rules are negotiable—or worse, performative.

This dynamic is not limited to overt use. Even silent digital behaviour—checking a smartwatch under the table, glancing at a phone during conversation—transmits cues about attention, urgency, and what truly matters. Research from human-computer interaction labs has demonstrated that children as young as four can accurately interpret the emotional valence of a parent's distraction: they can tell when the adult is absorbed, impatient, or checked out. This has social and emotional consequences. A child repeatedly interrupted by a parent's device will often disengage from attempts at connection, eventually mirroring that same inattentiveness in their own peer relationships.

Some may argue that this is the new normal—that all families must learn to coexist with technology and that occasional slips in attention are harmless. But the developmental window in which a child's baseline expectations are set is narrow and formative. Just as the dinner table shapes conversational fluency and bedtime routines structure emotional regulation, the unspoken rituals surrounding tech use become templates for how children will engage with the digital world. The question is not whether children will use devices—of course they will—but whether they will do so with a framework of intentionality or a model of compulsion.

This is where the notion of *screenwise parenting* comes into play. The goal is not to create a perfectly disciplined household with zero distractions, but rather to foster an environment in which technology is visible, discussed, and used with discernment. A parent who narrates their own choices—"I'm putting this away so I can really listen to you," or "I'm checking this message because Grandma is on her way"—models not just boundaries but values. These small declarations turn the opaque into the explicit. They teach not only what to do, but *why*.

Furthermore, the power of imitation extends to emotional tone. If a parent approaches tech with anxiety, reactivity, or obsession, those affective states become linked to devices in the child's mind. Conversely, if technology is integrated into the home as a tool for learning, communication, or creativity—rather than escape—then that orientation is likewise absorbed. This doesn't mean enforcing artificial positivity or shielding children from the pitfalls of the digital world. On the contrary, it requires honest conversations and visible decision-making. Children need to see adults grapple with distraction, choose to step away, and reflect openly on how digital habits affect well-being.

It is worth noting that imitation does not merely copy behaviour—it often exaggerates it. A child who sees their parent casually scrolling during moments of boredom may interpret that act as a necessary filler, eventually escalating it into an always-on expectation. Likewise, when children watch adults use tech to avoid discomfort—whether it's silence, conflict, or fatigue—they learn that those states are to be evaded rather than navigated. Attention span, frustration tolerance, and emotional self-regulation are all shaped by the adult response to mundane moments.

If the central insight is that children imitate more than they obey, then the practical implication is clear: to raise mindful digital citizens, adults must first become mindful digital models. This does not require perfection. In fact, the occasional misstep—followed by acknowledgement and course correction—can be more instructive than rigid adherence to an ideal. The point is not to create an artificial façade of control, but to live visibly with intention.

What emerges from this approach is a kind of quiet leadership. It rejects both authoritarianism and laissez-faire parenting in favour of *transparent example.* A child who watches a parent silence notifications before bedtime, who sees them resist the lure of an algorithmically curated rabbit hole, and who hears them articulate why these choices matter, gains more than compliance—they gain a script for their own autonomy. In time, these scripts become habits. And habits, unlike rules, travel with children into adolescence and adulthood, shaping not only how they use technology but how they relate to time, attention, and each other.

Ultimately, the habits we model are not just for our children—they are for ourselves. To live with presence is to honour the finite nature of our attention and to create space for the relationships we claim to value. In doing so, we don't merely teach children what to do; we invite them to become the kind of people who choose wisely when no one is watching.

## Designing Family Tech Agreements

One of the most paradoxical features of modern family life is the growing normalisation of technological overuse, despite almost universal discomfort with its effects. Parents lament their children's obsession with screens while simultaneously checking their own devices mid-conversation. Siblings retreat into separate digital silos even while sitting in the same room. Mealtimes, car rides, evenings—all spaces that once fostered shared experience—are increasingly perforated by digital interference. Yet for all the unease, very few families move from complaint to concrete change. Not because they don't care, but because they lack an organising framework. The notion of a "family tech agreement" remains unfamiliar to many, or else is dismissed as naïve, rigid, or bound to fail. But when well-conceived and collaboratively developed, such agreements offer one of the most practical, respectful, and resilient strategies for navigating technology in the home.

At its heart, a family tech agreement is not about control—it's about clarity. It does not aim to eliminate technology or treat it as an enemy, but to bring intentionality to its use. It replaces reactive policing with shared expectations. It transforms unspoken resentments and ad hoc rules into open dialogue. This shift is not cosmetic; it is foundational. Clarity fosters consistency, and consistency fosters trust. Children are far more likely to respect boundaries they helped define than ones imposed unilaterally. And adults are far less likely to default to frustration or hypocrisy when a mutually agreed framework exists.

Importantly, such agreements must begin not with children's behaviour but with family values. Before dictating time limits or banning certain apps, families must articulate what matters most to them. Do we value focused study and uninterrupted sleep? Do we cherish face-to-face connection during meals or protect certain hours for outdoor play? Do we believe in balancing digital entertainment with creative, offline pursuits? The specific content of a tech agreement should reflect these underlying priorities. Otherwise, the rules risk feeling arbitrary—rules for their own sake, rather than rules in service of something deeper.

One powerful approach is to conduct a "tech audit" together as a family. Not an accusatory inventory, but an honest accounting of how each person uses technology—what enhances their lives, what drains them, what habits feel compulsive versus conscious. Children, even young ones, can meaningfully participate in this process if the conversation is framed with curiosity and respect. Such audits often reveal surprising asymmetries: a parent who thinks they're modelling good behaviour may realise they're spending more time on email after hours than they imagined; a child glued to gaming may actually be seeking social connection they're not getting elsewhere. These discoveries humanise everyone involved. They defuse moral panic and make room for compassion.

Once this mutual understanding is established, the family can begin to co-create guidelines. These should be specific, realistic, and flexible—not aspirational manifestos destined to collapse under the weight of daily life. For example, rather than decree "no phones ever at dinner," a family might agree to keep devices off the table Monday through Thursday, with more relaxed rules on weekends. Or a household may designate "tech-free mornings" until school or work begins, to protect calm and focus. Older children might set their own app usage caps, revisited monthly. The key is that these decisions are made *with* children, not just *for* them. That collaborative spirit is what gives the agreement legitimacy.

Crucially, these agreements should not be static. As children mature, their needs, interests, and vulnerabilities shift. A policy that makes sense for a nine-year-old may be irrelevant—or insulting—to a sixteen-year-old. Family tech agreements must evolve through periodic review, ideally prompted not by conflict but by reflection. What's working? What feels outdated? What new challenges have arisen? These conversations model a core digital literacy skill: adaptability. They teach that the goal is not perfection, but responsiveness.

That said, a common objection arises at this point: won't kids simply manipulate these agreements to serve their desires? The answer is, sometimes, yes. But this is not a reason to abandon collaboration; it's a reason to make it more rigorous. A well-structured agreement doesn't simply grant freedom—it requires justification. If a teenager wants to stay up an hour later for online gaming with friends, the request must be accompanied by a plan for protecting sleep, balancing responsibilities, and monitoring mood. This develops not just compliance but metacognition—the ability to reflect on one's own habits, impulses, and trade-offs. That's a far more valuable outcome than mere obedience.

It's worth emphasising that enforcement still matters. Agreements without consequences are empty gestures. But enforcement need not be punitive. A breach of the agreement might trigger a reflective conversation rather than a punishment. For instance, if a child consistently violates agreed-upon limits, the family might revisit the reasons behind those limits—are they still appropriate? Was the agreement realistic? Is the breach a symptom of boredom, stress, or something else? This reframes enforcement as a relational process rather than a disciplinary one.

In homes with multiple children or blended families, the challenge of consistency becomes more pronounced. Age-appropriate differentiation is essential—what's fair for a ten-year-old will not look the same as what's fair for a seventeen-year-old. But even with differentiated rules, the *process* can remain consistent: transparency, collaboration, and mutual respect. When children see that rules are negotiated rather than dictated, and that fairness is rooted in need rather than uniformity, they are less likely to perceive double standards.

Some families may benefit from external scaffolding. Templates for tech agreements exist from reputable organisations like Common Sense Media or the American Academy of Paediatrics. These can provide a starting point but should never be applied verbatim. Each family is culturally, temperamentally, and logistically distinct. The value of a tech agreement lies not in its format but in its fit. In fact, families may choose to frame their agreements as values charters or digital mission statements rather than rulebooks. This flexibility allows the process to be shaped by identity rather than obligation.

The most overlooked element of effective family tech agreements is adult modelling. A parent who insists on no screens in bedrooms while secretly scrolling in their own bed sends a loud counter-message. The agreement is only as credible as the adults who honour it. Indeed, one of the most powerful clauses a family can include is a commitment to collective accountability. If anyone—adult or child—slips, they agree to name it, reflect on it, and repair. This practice normalises fallibility while reinforcing the agreement's shared ownership.

There is also a cultural dimension to consider. In many households, particularly those shaped by collectivist values or intergenerational living, tech norms are influenced by elders, visitors, or extended family. Creating agreements in these contexts may require broader conversation and negotiation. It may also require children to navigate multiple, sometimes conflicting, expectations—strict at home, lax at school; strict with one parent, lax with the other. This complexity should not be ignored. Instead, it should be named, explored, and used as an opportunity to teach discernment.

Above all, designing a family tech agreement is an exercise in intentional living. It compels families to ask: What kind of attention do we want to give each other? What kind of experiences do we want to protect? What kind of digital legacy are we creating—not just in terms of data or photos, but in terms of habits, rhythms, and norms? These are not small questions. They strike at the core of what it means to be a connected family in a connected age.

And the answer, ultimately, is not about rules, apps, or timers. It's about *culture*. A family tech agreement is not a solution to the problem of screens. It is a scaffold for building a culture of awareness, trust, and shared responsibility. It gives families the language, structure, and rhythm they need to stay human in a digital world—not by resisting technology, but by choosing how to live with it on purpose.

## Screens and Developmental Impact

Few topics in modern parenting ignite as much quiet anxiety as children's screen time. It is not only the sheer number of hours that concerns caregivers, but the feeling that something deeper and harder to articulate is at stake: the quality of attention, the texture of learning, the formation of character. Behind the statistics and headlines lies a more subtle reality: digital environments are not neutral vessels. They actively shape the mind—structuring how attention is deployed, how information is absorbed, and how thought is formed. And in children, whose cognitive, emotional, and neurological systems are still under construction, those effects are magnified.

To grasp the developmental impact of screens, we must begin by clarifying a foundational principle: *not all screen time is equal.* The phrase itself—screen time—is analytically unhelpful, lumping together radically different experiences: a toddler swiping randomly on YouTube; a ten-year-old coding a simple game; a teenager scrolling social media; a family watching a documentary together. The key variables are not just duration but *content*, *context*, *interactivity*, and *developmental stage.* A child's brain does not respond to a passive cartoon in the same way it responds to an interactive maths app, nor does a seven-year-old's experience of media parallel that of a fifteen-year-old. This nuance matters, and sweeping generalisations obscure more than they reveal.

Still, despite the diversity of digital experiences, certain patterns do emerge. One of the most consistently observed—and increasingly well-documented—effects of excessive screen exposure in young children is its interference with *sustained attention.* Human attention is a developmental achievement, not an innate trait. It must be practised, stretched, and scaffolded across early life. Activities that support this development are those that demand cognitive effort, tolerate slowness, and reward delayed gratification: listening to a story read aloud, engaging in imaginative play, building a structure with blocks. Screens—particularly those designed for rapid stimulation—often bypass these conditions. They flood the sensory field with novelty, colour, and reward, creating an attentional environment that is fast, fragmented, and passively received.

This has two consequences. First, children habituated to high-intensity digital input may struggle to engage with slower, less stimulating tasks—reading, puzzles, conversation—because those experiences feel underwhelming by comparison. Second, such exposure trains the brain to expect constant novelty, weakening the neural circuits involved in concentration and impulse control. Research from developmental neuroscience supports this concern: regions of the prefrontal cortex associated with attention regulation and executive function show different activation patterns in children with high screen use, though the direction of causality remains debated. What is clearer is the behavioural pattern—teachers and parents alike increasingly report children who are bright but scattered, capable of brief bursts of focus but easily derailed by distraction.

It would be intellectually dishonest, however, to paint all screens as corrosive. Interactive and well-designed digital experiences can, in fact, support learning—especially when aligned with developmental goals and mediated by an engaged adult. For instance, young children using apps that scaffold phonics or early numeracy—while supported by a caregiver who reinforces concepts—often show measurable academic gains. The problem arises not from the existence of screens, but from their *unbounded presence* in children's lives, and their frequent use as a default soother, babysitter, or boredom cure.

The issue is not that screens have no educational potential, but that they are often misaligned with what children developmentally need. Take boredom, for example. While often viewed as a problem to be eliminated, boredom is in fact a developmental crucible—a necessary condition for creativity, problem-solving, and self-directed exploration. When children are perpetually entertained by screens, they lose opportunities to develop these internal capacities. They become consumers of stimulation rather than creators of meaning.

Moreover, screen exposure intersects with sleep, which in turn shapes learning and memory consolidation. Multiple studies now show that screen use in the hour before bed disrupts melatonin release, delays sleep onset, and reduces sleep quality. For children and adolescents, whose brains undergo intensive synaptic pruning and memory consolidation during sleep, this erosion is not trivial. Sleep deprivation impairs attention, learning, emotional regulation, and long-term cognitive resilience. A child may technically be awake in class, but their working memory is depleted, their inhibitory control weakened, and their learning potential blunted.

Then there is the issue of co-viewing—or more often, the lack thereof. Screens can be enriching when they spark shared discussion or are embedded in social interaction. Yet in many households, screen time is solitary, passive, and unsupervised. Young children are left to navigate content ecosystems shaped by algorithms optimised not for developmental benefit but for engagement. In such environments, even educational content can give way to junk programming—because one video leads seamlessly, without friction, to the next. The child's agency is illusionary; the design is determinative.

The problem extends into school settings, where educational technologies are often introduced without adequate reflection on cognitive load or developmental readiness. Tablets and laptops promise personalised learning but can, in practice, splinter attention and externalise memory. When digital tools become the main conduit for learning, the risks include shallow processing, weakened handwriting fluency, reduced working memory, and an erosion of deep reading habits. Thought itself can become outsourced—fragmented across apps, tabs, and hyperlinks.

None of this means that children should be shielded entirely from screens. But it does demand a more intentional calibration of when, how, and why screens are used—especially during critical windows of development. Parents and educators should ask: Does this tool support focused attention, or splinter it? Does it promote creative expression or passive consumption? Is it designed to teach, or to addict? Is it a bridge to real-world engagement or a retreat from it? These are not rhetorical questions. They shape the developmental trajectory of the next generation.

Digital design itself is not neutral. Many apps and platforms explicitly weaponise psychological principles—variable rewards, infinite scroll, push notifications—to maximise user retention. Children are particularly susceptible to these dynamics because their impulse control systems are immature, and because they have less ability to exit addictive loops once entered. In this context, it is not enough to say "use responsibly." Children require scaffolding—both external (limits, routines, parental involvement) and internal (language for self-reflection, practice with delay of gratification). These are not just technical challenges; they are ethical ones.

There is also a profound equity issue at play. Wealthier families are increasingly adopting screen-light or screen-moderated parenting styles, hiring caregivers who engage children in face-to-face play, enrolling them in nature-based education, and enforcing device-free routines. Meanwhile, lower-income children often encounter screens earlier and more pervasively—not because their parents care less, but because economic and logistical constraints leave fewer alternatives. Without intervention, this disparity may widen the developmental divide, entrenching cognitive and behavioural gaps that persist into adolescence and beyond.

Finally, we must acknowledge the emotional layer of screen exposure. For many children, digital media is a site of identity formation, social belonging, and emotional coping. Cutting them off entirely may feel punitive, isolating, or developmentally regressive. The challenge, then, is not prohibition but integration: teaching children to inhabit the digital world with discernment, to reflect on their own habits, and to recognise when a tool is serving them versus when they are serving it.

Children do not need to be told that screens are "bad." What they need are adults who model thoughtful use, who set coherent boundaries, and who engage them in the why, not just the what. They need environments that support deep attention, meaningful conversation, and embodied play. And they need time—time to be bored, to build, to read, to wonder.

In the end, screens are not going away. Nor should they. The question is how we prepare children to navigate a world in which attention is both the most precious resource and the most targeted commodity. This preparation begins not with apps or filters, but with insight: understanding what growing minds need to thrive, and ensuring that our digital choices reflect, rather than erode, those needs. A developmental lens is not a luxury—it is a compass. Without it, we risk raising children who are technologically fluent but cognitively malnourished. With it, we have the opportunity to raise screenwise kids—curious, grounded, and equipped to live with technology without being led by it.

## Teaching Attention as a Skill

Children are not born with the ability to focus. The capacity to pay attention, resist distraction, and tolerate cognitive discomfort is a constructed competence, not a default setting. And yet, much of the modern world proceeds as if attention were either a genetic endowment or a personality trait—something children either have or don't. This assumption is not only inaccurate; it is developmentally negligent. *Attention is a skill*, and like any other skill—reading, swimming, riding a bike—it requires modelling, scaffolding, and repeated practice in supportive conditions. Without intentional cultivation, it atrophies. With it, children build the foundation for all meaningful learning, creativity, and emotional regulation.

What makes attention increasingly difficult to develop today is not that children have changed, but that their environments have. A child growing up in a screen-saturated world is rarely afforded the conditions in which deep attention naturally arises: unbroken time, quiet space, and emotionally regulated adults. Instead, they are frequently immersed in overstimulating media, fragmented routines, and households where adults themselves toggle between tasks at frenetic speed. Against this backdrop, a child's restlessness is not a moral failure or evidence of disorder—it is often a rational adaptation to a world that fragments attention by design.

Understanding this, parents must resist the temptation to outsource focus to punishment or praise. Telling a child to "concentrate more" is no more effective than telling them to "grow faster." The real work is environmental, relational, and iterative. Parents need to create the *conditions* in which attention is possible, model the *behaviours* that make it sustainable, and encourage the *metacognition* that makes it transferable. This is not a one-time intervention but a cultural orientation—one that begins in the home and echoes across a child's daily experience.

Start with environment. The architecture of attention is shaped by what is absent as much as by what is present. A quiet table with no devices in reach supports a different cognitive rhythm than a kitchen cluttered with alerts, background screens, and adult multitasking. When a child enters a space, they unconsciously ask: Is this a place where focus is normal, or where distraction is ambient? If every room is permeated by TV noise, phone pings, and interrupted conversation, attention becomes an uphill battle. Not because the child lacks willpower, but because their neurobiology is reacting—appropriately—to stimulus overload.

Equally important is time structure. Focus flourishes not in continuous intensity but in cycles: effort, rest, return. The Pomodoro technique—25 minutes of focused work followed by a 5-minute break—is a crude but illustrative example. For children, attention spans are naturally shorter, but the principle holds. Sprints of focused effort, when followed by intentional rest, are more effective than unbroken marathons of expectation. Unfortunately, many households reward sustained performance without acknowledging the need for recovery, creating patterns of cognitive burnout. Attention then becomes associated with pressure and depletion, rather than curiosity and engagement.

Perhaps most overlooked is boredom. In a culture allergic to boredom, children are taught—implicitly if not explicitly—that any moment of cognitive stillness must be filled. Waiting rooms, car rides, dinner tables—these are now commonly populated by tablets and phones that serve as pacifiers. But boredom is not a deficit to be patched; it is a developmental space to be inhabited. *Boredom is where the brain begins to wander, connect, and imagine.* When children are allowed to be bored—without immediate rescue from stimulation—they start to develop internal resources: imagination, self-direction, and yes, the muscle of attention itself.

This is not to suggest that children must be left alone to suffer boredom indefinitely. Rather, they need adults who understand its value and who can resist the urge to entertain them out of discomfort. When a child says, "I'm bored," the response need not be a list of activities. It can be: "That's okay. Sometimes good ideas start when nothing is happening." Such statements normalise the mental quiet from which attention can grow.

Modelling is just as critical. Children are acute observers of adult behaviour, and nowhere is this more consequential than with attention. A parent who glances at their phone mid-conversation, who habitually multitasks at the dinner table, or who cannot watch a film without second screening, sends a message louder than any lecture. That message is: *attention is optional, fragmented, and negotiable.* By contrast, an adult who listens fully, reads without interruption, and sets clear boundaries around screen time offers a living template of what sustained focus looks and feels like.

These patterns can be explicitly narrated, helping children connect action to intention. For example: "I'm putting my phone in the other room so I can really concentrate on reading this with you," or "Let's both turn our devices off so we can pay full attention to this game." Such moments teach children that attention is not automatic—it is a choice, one often supported by structure.

Beyond modelling, parents can also guide children to reflect on their own attentional states. A child who becomes aware of when and why their focus breaks is halfway to managing it. Simple questions help: "What makes it hard to concentrate on this?" "What helps you stay with it?" "Do you notice what your body feels like when you're really focused?" Over time, these queries foster metacognitive awareness—*the ability to think about one's own thinking*—which is essential for self-regulated learning.

But focus is not just a cognitive act; it is emotional and physical. Children who are anxious, overtired, or dysregulated will struggle to pay attention, regardless of motivation. Thus, building focus also means attending to foundational needs: sleep, nutrition, physical movement, and emotional connection. A child who feels safe, rested, and understood is more likely to sustain attention than one who is hungry, stressed, or lonely. This broader frame reminds us that attention is not a moral attribute or a sign of discipline; it is a holistic expression of wellbeing.

There are, of course, tools and techniques that can help. Mindfulness practices—adapted for children—have shown promising results in enhancing attentional control. Simple exercises like "listening to silence," breathing with awareness, or focusing on a single object can help train the brain to return to a point of focus when distracted. These exercises should be offered as experiments, not obligations—explorations of the mind's capacity rather than prescriptions for behaviour.

Educational systems also have a role to play, though they often undermine themselves by confusing busywork with engagement. Worksheets, flashcards, and endless test prep do little to train attention. What does? Deep, immersive learning experiences that invite curiosity, challenge, and agency. When children are engaged in a meaningful project, their focus becomes less about effort and more about flow. The role of the adult is not to coerce focus but to curate conditions where it naturally arises.

Yet even the best strategies fail without coherence. Parents cannot meaningfully ask children to attend deeply while their own lives are marked by constant distraction. Nor can they demand focus while allowing the home to be ruled by pinging devices and algorithmic attention traps. *Family life must model what it seeks to cultivate.* This does not require perfection—only consistency. Even a small set of shared norms—no phones at meals, screen-free mornings, reading time before bed—can create a rhythm where attention is both respected and reinforced.

Ultimately, the question is not whether children *can* learn to pay attention—they can. It is whether the adults in their lives are willing to slow down enough to make that learning possible. In a culture obsessed with speed and stimulation, this requires a kind of quiet courage. The courage to say: focus matters. Slowness has value. Boredom is fertile. And attention is not a luxury—it is the foundation of a well-lived life.

To teach attention is not to control children but to empower them. It is to gift them the internal infrastructure for learning, relating, and growing in a world that competes relentlessly for their eyes and minds. In doing so, we prepare them not merely to succeed in school, but to live in a way that is intentional, reflective, and grounded. Attention, once cultivated, becomes more than a skill. It becomes a way of being.

# Chapter 11
# Reclaiming Time, Rebuilding Self

Most people do not squander their time in grand, obvious gestures. They lose it in fractions so slight they barely register: a minute waiting for the kettle, ten minutes scrolling through videos that teach nothing, half an hour replying to messages that could have waited, an hour lost bouncing between tabs in pursuit of focus that never materialises. By the end of a day, the erosion seems trivial. Over a year, it accumulates into something foundational. What slips away is not merely minutes, but the scaffolding of one's inner life. Time spent without intention slowly eclipses the self.

We tend to treat time as a backdrop, a neutral stage on which life unfolds. Yet it is far more intimate. Time is the raw material of existence—shaped by attention, etched into memory. Unlike money or energy, it cannot be banked, paused, or reclaimed. Losing an hour to mindless scrolling is not neutral; it is a quiet act of self-erasure, an exchange of something irretrievable for something forgettable. The disquieting truth is that this pattern has become normal.

What sets our era apart is not the presence of distraction, but its architecture. Digital platforms are meticulously engineered to exploit cognitive vulnerabilities, delivering dopamine rewards in response to behaviours they themselves cultivate. To believe that one is "choosing" time online is to ignore the subtle choreography of nudges and anticipation embedded in these systems. Attention, once private, has become infrastructure—harvested, monetised, optimised for purposes other than our own.

Yet this chapter does not begin with blame. It begins with awareness. The question is not perfection, but presence: presence with one's habits, patterns of attention, and inherited assumptions about what constitutes a "productive" or "normal" day. The goal is not self-denial, but self-direction. What becomes possible when time is reclaimed from compulsion and reinvested with intention?

Start with an audit. Not of your calendar, but of your lived hours. Where do your days go from dawn to dusk? Which activities expand your sense of self, and which contract it? This is not a moral judgement on screen time, but a careful observation of consequence. A ninety-second news headline may inform; ninety minutes of passive scrolling often leaves behind emptiness, envy, or agitation. Repeated over days and weeks, this residue sets the baseline of experience.

It is worth distinguishing between time that is full and time that is filled. A walk with a friend, an afternoon absorbed in a novel, an hour of deep work—these fill time with substance. Screen time often fills hours without nourishment. It occupies, but it does not satisfy. In a world that rewards the appearance of activity over meaningful engagement, it is easy to mistake busyness for life itself.

More subtly, the digital economy offers endless micro-escapes from the discomfort that signals growth. Solitude, once the soil of thought, is now avoided. Boredom, formerly the spark of imagination, is treated as a problem to solve immediately. Both states, however, are essential. Solitude allows integration; boredom cultivates creativity. Without them, clarity, insight, and originality are diminished.

The discomfort of unoccupied moments is not a flaw—it is a feature. Allowing boredom to unfold is to open a dialogue with the mind. In that stillness, trivial impulses recede, subtler instincts arise. Decisions to walk, journal, call a friend, or start a project emerge not in opposition to distraction, but in the absence of it. An uninterrupted mind reveals its own rhythm.

Children once discovered this naturally. Long, unstructured afternoons produced forts, stories, and inventions. Adults must relearn this art—not to maximise productivity, but to reclaim humanity. To honour boredom is to trust that the mind can discover what is worthy without constant external prompts.

Reclaiming time is never a one-off gesture; it is a continual, deliberate responsibility. Custodianship of time requires curating inputs, observing patterns, and making hard trade-offs. It involves recognising that constant engagement often erodes depth and asking not just, "What am I doing?" but, "Who am I becoming as I do this?"

This perspective shifts everything. Platforms may entertain, inform, even inspire. Yet if usage leaves one anxious, reactive, fragmented, or numb, the net effect is not neutral. Custodianship demands courage: the willingness to walk away from platforms misaligned with values and to restructure routines in service of something greater than efficiency.

Custodianship is not asceticism. It is not a call to reject technology wholesale. It is a reframing of one's relationship to time to reflect identity and intention. For some, this may take the form of digital sabbaths—hours or days without screens. For others, it may mean returning to analogue practices: reading paper books, writing by hand, cooking without background noise. The particular methods matter less than the principle: time should be inhabited, not merely spent.

Paradoxically, disconnecting rarely feels like deprivation. It brings abundance: more energy, sharper thought, stronger memory, richer relationships, and space to remember what matters. This is not nostalgia—it is neurobiology. Minds renew in silence, not saturation. Identity is shaped by what one chooses when no external curator dictates attention.

In reclaiming time, the insight becomes clear: what we need is rarely more content, but more context—perspective, agency, and space to listen to ourselves. This chapter offers practical guidance for navigating that reclamation: tracking where time flows, distinguishing nourishment from distraction, recovering solitude and wonder, and stepping into the role of steward over our most finite resource.

Not because it is fashionable, but because your time is your life. To reclaim it is to begin the work of rebuilding yourself.

## Where Your Time Went

It is not uncommon to reach the end of a day, week, or even year with the disquieting sense that something essential has slipped away—but it is harder to name exactly what. The modern experience of time is not characterised by obvious loss, but by slow diffusion. Hours disappear not in moments of crisis but in small, cumulative surrenders to platforms optimised to capture them. Most people are not squandering time in open defiance of their values; they are bleeding it invisibly in a state of cognitive drift.

The most reliable sign of time loss is not a blank calendar—it is a full one, densely packed yet devoid of memory. People often describe days that felt busy but produced nothing memorable. The explanation lies not in laziness or poor planning but in a quiet hijacking of attention that fractures time into unrecoverable fragments. A few minutes here to check a message, a short scroll before a meeting, an autoplayed video late at night. These actions are individually trivial but collectively monumental. What's been taken is not just time, but coherence.

The human mind is not naturally segmented into dozens of micro-attentions. It craves narrative, purpose, and flow—elements difficult to sustain when attention is continually rerouted. Yet this fragmentation has become the norm. According to a 2023 study from RescueTime, knowledge workers toggle between apps over 1,100 times per day, often without completing a single intentional task in between. This is not a benign statistic. *What we attend to repeatedly becomes our cognitive environment.* Over time, the mental noise generated by constant switching diminishes not only output, but interior clarity.

Technology is not neutral in this process. It is designed to monetise attention by engineering compulsion. Features like infinite scroll, notification batching, autoplay, algorithmic feeds, and streak mechanics are not accidental conveniences—they are behavioural levers. When users report feeling as though they've lost time online, it is because they have. Their sense of agency has been bypassed by systems that exploit neural shortcuts for profit. It is no coincidence that many people can recall the last series they binge-watched but struggle to name the last hour they spent thinking deeply or being fully present.

An honest audit begins not with shame but with observation. This is a radical act in a world that thrives on unreflective use. Consider

a typical day and ask, with precision:
– How often do you reach for your phone without a clear reason?
– How frequently do "quick checks" spiral into unintended consumption?
– Which apps provide genuine value, and which ones merely pacify discomfort?
– When during the day are you most vulnerable to distraction, and why?

These questions are not philosophical indulgences; they are diagnostic tools. *Awareness of use precedes intentionality of use.* Many individuals experience compulsive tech habits not because they lack discipline, but because they've never mapped those habits onto their personal goals. The brain, like any system, follows what is repeated. Left unchecked, it will build routines around short-term ease, not long-term meaning.

There is a subtle but critical distinction between use and loss. Not all screen time is wasted. Some apps facilitate creativity, connection, even calm. The problem arises when time spent on devices begins to override time spent with intention. Psychologist Mihaly Csikszentmihalyi, in his foundational work on flow states, noted that optimal experience arises when individuals engage in structured, meaningful challenges. Very few digital platforms are structured to support such states. Instead, they interrupt them. The average smartphone user touches their device 2,617 times a day, a number that undermines any ambition toward deep work or sustained reflection.

Consider how rarely digital tools respect the contours of human attention. Push notifications arrive regardless of context, treating all moments as equally interruptible. Email inboxes, designed decades ago as asynchronous communication tools, now behave like live chat. Social platforms, meant to simulate connection, reward outrage and novelty over truth or nuance. When people say they "don't have time" to read, create, rest, or reflect, what they often mean is that their attention has been conscripted elsewhere—without their full consent.

Compulsive tech use does not only displace productive time. It distorts perception. An hour lost to scrolling does not merely replace an hour of writing, thinking, or walking—it replaces the *possibility* of insight, engagement, or presence. This is why screen audits matter. They are not about reducing hours per se; they are about restoring *access to choice.* Without visibility, habits harden into default settings that define entire years.

One powerful practice is to track time use retroactively for one week. Not as an act of surveillance, but of reclamation. Write down what you did every 30 to 60 minutes throughout the day, noting both activity and level of intention. Most people discover that much of their day unfolds in reactive patterns, shaped more by external cues than internal priorities. This data is not just revealing; it is reorienting. It reconnects individuals with their agency by showing them where it has quietly atrophied.

Contrary to popular assumption, distraction is not the opposite of focus. *Distraction is the erosion of priority.* It replaces deliberate action with convenience, often masked as engagement. The antidote is not rigid discipline or self-flagellation, but design. Environments can be structured to support rather than sabotage focus. This includes deleting apps that serve no constructive purpose, silencing notifications during deep work hours, creating tech-free zones in the home, and establishing recurring periods of full disconnection. These actions are not dramatic. They are infrastructural.

Restoring time is not about turning back the clock—it is about reclaiming authorship. The cost of unchecked digital habits is not measured in missed hours alone, but in *missed identity formation.* Every hour shaped by algorithmic drift is an hour not spent discovering what one thinks, believes, builds, or becomes. This is not an abstraction. Over time, identity is composed of thousands of such hours. The danger is not that tech use makes people passive; it is that it makes passivity feel normal.

Those who regain clarity about where their time went often experience a form of grief—grief for the years spent reacting instead of choosing. But grief is not useless. It can become fuel. The point is not to dwell in regret, but to see time as a renewable force—one that, when harnessed, can transform not just productivity, but self-perception. When people begin to treat time as a mirror of their values rather than a container to be filled, they act differently. They say no more often. They move slower. They engage with depth.

A final reflection: most people do not need more time. They need *access to the time they already have.* That access has been obscured by systems that monetise attention by dislocating intention. But it can be restored. And when it is, the result is not merely better focus or higher output—it is a re-encounter with what it feels like to be fully alive.

## Time Freedom vs. Time Fillers

Not all time is created equal. A calendar hour may be fixed, but its experiential value varies drastically depending on how it is used—and, more importantly, whether it is consciously chosen or unconsciously filled. Modern life is awash with busyness, but most of it is *cognitive clutter*, not purposeful living. The distinction between time freedom and time fillers is not trivial; it is the difference between agency and drift, presence and dissociation, meaning and motion for motion's sake.

Time freedom does not refer to idle leisure or the romanticised ideal of empty schedules. It is not about doing nothing, nor is it synonymous with "free time" as marketed in wellness content. It is the state of having one's *internal priorities drive the use of time*, rather than external forces or algorithmic persuasion. A person experiencing time freedom is not merely off the clock—they are in alignment. Their activities match their values. Their attention is not perpetually hijacked by digital diversions or reactive obligations. Crucially, they are aware of how and why they spend their time the way they do.

By contrast, time fillers are those stretches of activity that soothe, distract, or occupy without satisfying. They are the default settings of a hyperstimulated culture: a compulsive scroll between tasks, ambient television in the background, the reflexive checking of messages, or even calendar slots crammed with meetings that serve no strategic purpose. Time fillers feel active—they may even feel productive—but they are largely hollow. What makes them insidious is their plausibility. A person immersed in them can appear engaged while remaining fundamentally disengaged from themselves.

This distinction is not philosophical posturing; it has measurable psychological effects. A 2022 study published in the *Journal of Experimental Psychology* found that individuals who structured their time around internally chosen goals reported significantly higher life satisfaction than those whose schedules were externally driven—even when both groups performed the same types of tasks. It is not the task itself, but the *ownership* of the task, that creates meaning. Time freedom is psychological first, practical second. It begins with sovereignty over attention.

One of the challenges in reclaiming this sovereignty is that digital environments are optimised for frictionless consumption. They do not demand intention; they invite reaction. The next video plays automatically, the next notification pings unprompted, the next scroll delivers another flash of novelty. There is no built-in pause for reflection. As a result, people increasingly spend their time in *passive acceleration*—moving quickly without directing the motion. The feeling is not one of calm or joy but of being always behind, always catching up, always wondering what just happened.

This has profound implications for how we understand productivity. In most contemporary settings, productivity is treated as a metric of throughput—how many emails sent, meetings attended, hours worked. But when this activity is examined closely, a significant portion of it reveals itself as filler: low-impact output driven by urgency rather than importance. Time fillers masquerade as obligations but often have no real consequence. Time freedom, by contrast, produces *intentional output*—fewer actions, but more aligned with long-term vision.

The problem is compounded by cultural narratives that conflate busyness with virtue. There is an unspoken valorisation of the packed schedule, the exhausted reply, the multi-tasking lifestyle. To say "I'm slammed" is, in many circles, a status signal. It implies relevance, indispensability, even moral worth. But there is growing evidence that this model is neither effective nor sustainable. Burnout rates have soared not just because people work hard, but because they work *mindlessly hard*—filling time without renewing meaning.

Understanding time freedom requires a shift in mental framing. It is not about having less to do; it is about doing fewer things better and more consciously. This does not mean rejecting obligations or eschewing structure. It means *interrogating the function* of each obligation. Does this meeting serve a strategic purpose, or is it an inherited norm? Does this platform nourish connection, or merely stimulate comparison? Does this routine anchor you in the day, or pull you through it numbly?

One illustrative framework comes from behavioural economist Sendhil Mullainathan, who distinguishes between "time poverty" and "attention poverty." Time poverty is an objective lack of hours; attention poverty is the inability to focus the hours available. Most modern individuals experience the latter. They may technically have leisure time, but it is splintered by interruptions, drained by decision fatigue, or shaped entirely by consumption habits they did not consciously choose. *Time fillers flourish in attention poverty.*

To reclaim time freedom, it is essential to develop a practice of intentional scheduling—not merely putting events in a calendar, but actively *curating* what earns space on it. A useful method is to colour-code entries not by type (meeting, exercise, social), but by purpose: creation, connection, restoration, administration. This simple act of classification reveals patterns. It makes visible the ratio of reactive versus generative activity. From there, one can begin to rebalance.

Equally important is the practice of strategic subtraction. Time freedom is less about adding more meaningful activities and more about *removing what does not matter.* The great unspoken truth of productivity is that most to-do lists are built to avoid discomfort—not to advance value. Meetings replace difficult decisions. Inbox zero becomes a proxy for progress. Social media scrolling simulates interaction without the risk of true presence. Choosing not to engage with these fillers is a form of discipline, not deprivation.

There are counterarguments worth acknowledging. Some might suggest that filler time is necessary for relaxation, that not every moment must be purposeful. This is true—but it misses the core point. Time freedom is not about constant intensity. It includes rest, but rest that is *chosen*, not default. Watching a film as a shared ritual is not the same as collapsing into YouTube recommendations for three hours because nothing else feels tolerable. The difference is not in content, but in consciousness.

Likewise, the appeal of time fillers often stems from emotional avoidance. They anaesthetise boredom, loneliness, or ambiguity. In doing so, they protect the psyche temporarily—but they also prevent the deeper self-examination required to evolve. Boredom, properly understood, is not a problem to be solved, but a signal to be explored. It points to misalignment between stimulation and meaning. When boredom is simply repressed with filler activity, it loses its function as an inner compass.

If time fillers are the cultural default, time freedom must be deliberately designed. This includes building margins between tasks, declining invitations that dilute focus, and creating *off-platform zones* in one's home and day. It means treating attention as a scarce resource, not a renewable one. And it means normalising periods of quiet—not as unproductive voids, but as fertile ground for insight, reflection, and recalibration.

Ultimately, the goal is not perfection but proportion. Everyone will have some filler time; the issue is whether it dominates. The aspiration is not to optimise every moment but to ensure that one's time architecture supports—rather than obscures—what matters. When individuals transition from filler to freedom, the change is often subtle but profound. They begin to experience time not as a scarcity to be squeezed, but as a space to inhabit. They speak more slowly. They notice more. They act with calm resolve rather than frenetic urgency.

And perhaps most importantly, they stop mistaking movement for momentum.

## Recovering Boredom and Solitude

It is a curious paradox of modern life that while most people claim to crave peace and quiet, they simultaneously recoil from boredom and avoid solitude at all costs. In the age of infinite content and persistent connectivity, even a momentary lull is treated as a problem to be solved. Waiting in a queue, riding in a lift, sitting in traffic—none of these intervals are allowed to remain unoccupied. They are quickly filled with a reflexive glance at a phone, a scroll through updates, a tap into entertainment. Boredom, once considered an ordinary feature of human experience, has become intolerable. Yet its absence may be silently eroding something essential: our capacity for creativity, depth, and self-renewal.

The pathological fear of boredom is not merely cultural; it is now biologically conditioned. Numerous studies in neuroscience have confirmed that the repeated use of digital media—especially platforms designed for variable rewards, such as social media feeds or mobile games—alters the brain's dopamine circuits. Novelty becomes a neurological expectation, not an occasional delight. This has profound consequences for how attention functions. It trains the brain to seek stimulation over reflection, reaction over imagination. The result is a subtle but pervasive restlessness: the inability to be where one is, with what is.

Boredom, in its uncorrupted form, is not a deficit. It is a *signal.* It arises when the mind is under-stimulated *by its current input* and is ready to generate its own stimulation from within. It is the quiet nudge that precedes a creative insight, the pause before an idea emerges, the silence into which thought expands. When boredom is routinely bypassed, the space for this inner generation shrinks. The individual becomes dependent on external content to feel alive. Over time, this erodes not just creativity, but autonomy. A mind that cannot tolerate boredom is a mind that must always be fed.

Solitude, too, has been mischaracterised. In popular discourse, it is often conflated with loneliness—a deficit state. But solitude is not absence. It is presence with oneself. It is the psychological condition in which self-reflection, value clarification, and mental integration become possible. Historically, artists, philosophers, and spiritual practitioners have sought solitude deliberately, not as escape, but as a crucible. It allows one to hear internal signals without distortion. Without solitude, identity becomes porous, reactive, constantly shaped by the opinions and validations of others.

There is mounting empirical support for this perspective. A longitudinal study from the University of Virginia found that participants who were asked to sit quietly without any distractions for fifteen minutes often chose to administer mild electric shocks to themselves rather than remain alone with their thoughts. This is not a trivial finding. It suggests that the modern mind is so acclimated to external input that internal experience feels alien, even threatening. But that discomfort is not evidence of pathology—it is evidence of disuse. Like an atrophied muscle, the capacity for generative thought must be exercised to be retained.

From a developmental lens, boredom and solitude are essential for children as well. Child psychologists have long observed that unstructured time is where creativity flourishes. It is in the "I'm bored" moments that imaginative play often begins. Yet many well-meaning parents, anxious to optimise their child's time or avoid their discomfort, fill every gap with planned activities or digital pacifiers. The child learns to fear stillness, to associate it with lack. Over time, this can weaken their tolerance for ambiguity, undermine intrinsic motivation, and diminish their ability to self-regulate attention.

This is not an argument for asceticism. It is not a call to eliminate entertainment or connection. Rather, it is a call to *rebalance*. To reintroduce the lost art of doing nothing. To sit with oneself not as punishment, but as practice. Consider, for example, the experience of walking without headphones. What thoughts emerge? What patterns return? These are not mere curiosities—they are clues to what the mind truly values when left unmanipulated.

The philosopher Blaise Pascal famously wrote, "All of humanity's problems stem from man's inability to sit quietly in a room alone." That statement may seem hyperbolic, but it contains a grain of psychological truth. The constant fleeing from boredom and solitude often masks deeper anxieties: fear of purposelessness, fear of self-evaluation, fear of insignificance. But avoidance does not resolve these tensions—it only buries them beneath distraction. When people reacquaint themselves with the capacity to be alone, without input, they often find not emptiness, but clarity.

There are practical strategies to begin this reacquaintance. One is the deliberate design of input-free intervals in daily life. These are not merely screen-free, but stimulation-free. No podcast during the commute. No music while tidying the house. No checking headlines while sipping morning coffee. These micro-solitudes function as emotional decompression chambers. They create perceptual whitespace—mental room in which ideas can stretch, feelings can surface, and attention can reorient itself around the present.

Another is the ritualisation of solitude. This means making space for it not as an afterthought, but as a recurring appointment. It could be a morning journaling practice, an evening walk, or even a half-day retreat away from devices. The key is consistency and intentionality. Over time, these spaces become less threatening and more nourishing. They become a *resource*, not a void.

It is also worth addressing the fear that boredom leads to stagnation. The opposite is often true. Many creative breakthroughs are preceded by periods of boredom. It is in the slack, not the surge, that new mental configurations arise. Psychologists have described this as the "default mode network" of the brain—a neural system that becomes active when the mind is at rest. This is when autobiographical thinking, future planning, and idea synthesis occur. Constant task engagement suppresses this mode. By reclaiming boredom, one reopens access to this cognitive depth.

Of course, not all boredom is beneficial. Chronic understimulation caused by poverty, trauma, or structural oppression is not the same as voluntary disengagement. Here, boredom becomes existential, not fertile. This distinction matters. What is being argued for is *chosen boredom*—space voluntarily opened within a safe and structured life, not boredom imposed by deprivation. The former fosters resilience and creativity; the latter can erode them.

Rebuilding a tolerance for boredom and solitude is not a one-time shift. It is a developmental process. The first stages may feel frustrating, even pointless. But with repetition, they yield something increasingly rare: the ability to *generate meaning without input.* That is perhaps the defining skill of a fulfilled mind. It is what allows people to create rather than consume, to initiate rather than react, to be content not because of what surrounds them, but because of what sustains them internally.

In reclaiming boredom and solitude, people do not regress—they evolve. They step out of the hamster wheel of hyper-engagement and rediscover a fundamental truth: *being is enough to begin.* From that beginning, everything else—attention, creativity, well-being—can grow.

## Becoming a Custodian of Your Days

The most important resource any person possesses is not money, data, or even knowledge. It is time. Yet time, unlike other resources, is not something one can accumulate, store, or regenerate. It flows only in one direction and disappears as it moves. What makes this even more consequential is the quiet fact that *most of our time is not taken, but given away.* It is not stolen in dramatic fashion—it slips through unnoticed in distracted gestures, unconscious habits, compulsive scrolling, and low-stakes busyness. It is not lost all at once, but dissipated in fragments, until the day arrives when a person begins to wonder not just where the hours went, but whether they ever truly owned them.

To become a custodian of one's days is to shift from passive experience to deliberate stewardship. It is to recognise that attention is not merely a cognitive function, but an existential vote. Every moment of attention given is a moment of self conferred. What we attend to becomes our experience; what we repeat becomes our identity. And in a culture of digital saturation—where every platform is designed to monetise attention and every app is engineered to anticipate and exploit psychological vulnerabilities—custodianship becomes a radical act of autonomy.

One of the most destabilising effects of the attention economy is not just how it fragments concentration, but how it obscures value.

When everything is vying for your time, the default becomes *reactivity* rather than *intention.* People begin to measure their days not by what they moved closer to, but by how much they managed to get through. Productivity replaces purpose. Noise replaces clarity. In this landscape, reclaiming one's time is not about optimisation; it is about orientation. The central question is not "How can I do more?" but *"What is worth doing at all?"*

Many modern individuals find themselves chronically busy, yet privately adrift. The calendar is full, but the heart is empty. The inbox overflows, but the mind is undernourished. Busyness, in this context, becomes not a marker of importance, but of evasion. It allows people to avoid the deeper, more difficult inquiries: What matters to me? What am I becoming through the way I spend my time? These are not rhetorical questions; they are navigational instruments. Without them, people risk living lives of default—shaped more by algorithmic suggestions than conscious decisions.

The call to stewardship is not a call to withdraw from the world. It is not an argument for technophobia, monastic withdrawal, or the romanticisation of pre-digital life. It is, rather, an invitation to *reclaim authorship* of how time is spent and experienced. It demands discernment: the ability to differentiate between what is urgent and what is important, between what is merely stimulating and what is truly nourishing. That discernment is only possible when individuals pause long enough to remember that attention is not free. It is always paid—if not by the self, then by the self's potential.

To become a custodian of your days requires not simply better time management techniques, but a shift in worldview. One must begin to see time not as a blank canvas to be filled, but as a finite domain to be honoured. Every day is not a container to be packed with maximum efficiency; it is a landscape to be shaped with intention. This requires moving beyond external markers of success—metrics, notifications, productivity apps—and cultivating internal ones: clarity, presence, coherence.

There is a profound difference between a schedule and a life. Many people maintain highly optimised schedules that nonetheless leave them spiritually depleted. This paradox emerges when time is treated solely as a logistical problem rather than an ethical one. To steward one's time is not merely to allocate it better; it is to align it with what one values. This requires periodic examination—an audit not just of tasks completed, but of whether those tasks served one's core commitments. Were the most meaningful conversations avoided because of busyness? Were quiet intervals sacrificed to dopamine loops? Did the day move the self forward—or simply keep it distracted?

Custodianship also involves recognising the cumulative effects of micro-choices. A person may not consciously choose to give two hours to a platform, but they may tap a dozen times for three minutes each—never once considering the opportunity cost. When attention is fragmented, time does not *feel* lost, even as it *is*. One of the central strategies of digital design is precisely this: to minimise friction so thoroughly that the user forgets they are choosing at all. The response to this cannot merely be self-discipline; it must include systemic awareness. One must learn to recognise design patterns that erode agency and then build counter-practices that restore it.

Some individuals respond to this dilemma with drastic moves—digital detoxes, deleted accounts, minimalist calendars. These can be helpful, even necessary. But sustainable custodianship is not built on short-term abstinence; it is built on *long-term attention literacy*. It involves building a relationship with one's time that is not reactive, but reflective. What does it mean, for instance, to start the day not by reaching for the phone, but by orienting to a chosen aim? What shifts when the final hour before bed is protected from inputs and given to integration? These are not just productivity hacks—they are acts of self-respect.

Importantly, stewardship of time is not a solo project. Culture shapes habits, and habits shape culture. When workplaces normalise constant availability, when social expectations presume instant replies, when parenting models conflate screen time with peace, the individual faces an uphill battle. Yet individual custodianship has ripple effects. A person who lives deliberately gives others permission to do the same. A team that respects focused time reshapes its own norms. A parent who guards their evenings redefines family life. Stewardship, then, becomes not just a personal ethic, but a cultural contribution.

There will always be competing demands. Children need feeding, deadlines loom, emergencies arise. The goal is not to eliminate unpredictability, but to *build an inner structure* that can flex without collapsing. That structure comes from prioritising alignment over volume, coherence over coverage. When time reflects values, even the busy days feel inhabited. When time is driven by default, even empty days feel full of noise.

To be a custodian of your days is not to win time, but to *honour it.* It is to meet each hour as a participant, not a consumer. It is to remember, in a culture of acceleration, that slowness can be a form of clarity. In a culture of performance, that silence can be a form of strength. And in a culture of distraction, that presence can be a revolutionary act.

The final metric of a life well lived will not be how much one achieved, but whether the self doing the achieving was present, integrated, and awake. Custodianship is the practice that makes that presence possible—not just once, but repeatedly, hour by hour, day by day. What one does with their days is, ultimately, what one does with their life. There is no higher calling than to live it on purpose.

## About the Author

Elias Ward is a writer and researcher obsessed with the hidden costs of modern life. With a background in digital behavior, design ethics, and contemplative practice, he helps readers navigate the silent forces shaping their choices—especially those shaped by screens. His work explores the intersection of technology and intentional living, offering tools that are as practical as they are philosophical. Elias lives largely offline by design, choosing deep work, long walks, and screen-free dinners over the dopamine loops of modern life. This book reflects his belief that attention is our last great frontier—and reclaiming it may be the most human act left.